R. Atkinson Fox
Book Two

RITA C. MORTENSON

Cover Design: David Dilley
Interior Layout: David Dilley

ISBN # 0-89538-002-1

Published by:
L-W Book Sales
P.O.Box 69
Gas City,IN 46933

This book is respectfully and lovingly dedicated to:

The memory of my mother whose courage during a six-year battle with throat and lung cancer stands as eloquent memorial and living inspiration.

My best friend and Number One Fox Hunter: My husband, Bob.

R. Atkinson Fox 1860–1935

CONTENTS

NOTES

INTRODUCTION

R. Atkinson Fox was born in Toronto on December 11, 1860. He was one of four sons born to Sarah Atkinson and William Henry Fox, a Presbyterian minister. Little is known of RAF's early life except that he worked in Toronto as an artist and portrait painter from 1877 to 1884. In 1885, he worked for T. Lyons, a stained-glass manufacturer.

Fox apparently moved to the United States between 1885 and 1890. Auctions of his work were held in New York in 1891, and in Boston in 1893. The Boston catalog lists his address as New York. He exhibited with the Philadelphia Art Club in 1897 and 1898. The Philadelphia directory shows his address as 1308 Walnut Street, Philadelphia, for 1900 to 1902.

Fox married Anna Gaffney in 1903, when he was almost forty-three and she was twenty-five. The marriage license, issued September 24, 1903, lists RAF's address as "Penn. St., Woodbury, N.J.," and Anna's as "1634 Francis St., Philadelphia."

Little is known of Anna's background. Both her parents were born in Ireland and came to the United States as farmers. Anna was born in Germantown, Pennsylvania on April 7, 1878.

Between 1904 and 1920, RAF and Anna became the parents of eight children, five of whom are still living at this writing. The family lived at several addresses in New Jersey before moving to Chicago in the early 1920's. RAF's final address was 4450 North Lincoln in Chicago, the home where he died January 24, 1935. Anna remained active and in good health until her death in Chicago in May, 1964. As complete a biography as was possibly to construct from known records, interviews and correspondence appears in Book One.

The project known loosely and affectionately as "Fox Hunt" was born in the spring of 1980. It grew from my frustration as a writer, researcher, and antique dealer, with the lack of information on the artist whose prints were being avidly sought by so many collectors. A small ad in the "Antique Trader" brought correspondence from collectors across the country.

The high point of "Fox Hunt" came in the fall of 1982, when I finally made contact with RAF's surviving children. Seven "Trader" articles preceded publication of R. Atkinson Fox: His Life and Work in 1985 (Book One). An updated edition of Book One was published by L-W Book Sales in 1991.

The manuscript for Book One had no sooner arrived at the publisher than the editors were talking to me about Book Two. I couldn't deal with the notion at all. My husband kept teasing me. A new photo or some gem of information would come in and I'd say, "I wonder if I can still get this into the book."

"Better save it for Book Two," Bob would suggest, and I'd just shake my head. Three hundred and twenty prints appeared in Book One; I couldn't imagine that another collection of that size was still out there. Finally, one day, I asked him, "Do you have a good, sturdy box that would fit here, on the corner of my desk?" "For Book Two?" he asked. I nodded, doubtfully. "I'll find one," he said, laughing. And he did.

• •

As you read this book, please keep in mind that where I use the collective pronoun, "We," I am referring not only to the members of "Fox Hunt," but also to anyone who might have written to me. The personal "I" usually refers to my own efforts or opinions.

For your convenience, prints are arranged according to subject matter. A detailed table of contents is included to aid readers in locating and identifying certain prints.

Illustrations are numbered consecutively: Fig. 1 through Fig. 688. The numbers that appear in parentheses are "Fox List" numbers. The "Fox List" continues to be compiled in an effort to facilitate communication between collectors and dealers. Each print has been numbered in the order in which it came to my attention. Numbers that appear directly before or after the title or the publisher's name are usually the publisher's inventory or identification numbers. They are not necessarily of concern to the reader wishing to simply locate and identify a print.

Looking at the "Index By Fox-List Number," you will notice that some numbers are missing. Sometimes this is because a print has been inadvertently double-listed, and the offending or second number has been eliminated. In some cases, such as the Prudential children, prints have been "stripped" of their Fox-list status for one reason or another--usually additional information. In one case, I simply skipped a number. There is no F.L. #566 because my brain skipped and the list went from #565 to #567.

This book, also, is not complete. Until the moment of writing these introductory words, I have continued to list and add prints as new finds have arrived. During the time it will take to complete the price guide and ship the manuscript, the mail will undoubtedly bring new finds that cannot be included. "Fox Hunt," the newsletter, will continue to communicate such finds to its subscribers. However, there surely can't be enough new finds out there for a Book Three!

REPRODUCTIONS

Every print illustrated in this book is in one sense a reproduction. That is, it was "reproduced" from an original painting. Collectors consider a print "original" when it exists <u>in the form for which it was originally intended and used</u>--a magazine cover, advertising fan, calendar, etc.

Unfortunately, and inevitably I guess, modern reproductions of RAF's work are currently on the market. And it isn't even the professional repro dealer that is causing the worst problems--at least we can keep track of what they are offering. The biggest problem is that the color laser copier has made reproducing a print as easy as carrying it down to your local printer's office, business-supply store, or maybe your own office. I have been told that some unscrupulous sellers will even dip a print in a weak coffee or tea solution to give it that "old" look.

It is difficult, if not impossible, to protect against such reproductions. One way is to examine the print under magnification. Can you see foxing, water stains, or other slight damage? Such damage should be <u>on</u> the print, but in case of a copy, it will appear <u>in</u> the print. If the color copy has not been tampered with, the margins and back will appear unsuitably "white." Of course, as always, your best protection is to do business only with reputable dealers who will guarantee that the merchandise they sell is genuine, original and old.

PHOTOGRAPHS & CREDITS

In preparing this book it was not possible to bring all the prints to one location to be photographed under uniform lighting by a professional photographer. The prints and paintings represented in this book belong to collectors all over the United States. Some <u>have</u> been photographed by professionals. In some cases, a relative or neighbor with a "good camera" has lent a helping hand. And some prints have simply been leaned against a chair or tree and snapped by whatever camera was available. L-W Book Sales deserves thanks for recognizing that it is more important for you to see a photograph of a print than to omit it because it fails to meet their usual high standards. Again, I wish to thank all who sent photographs or prints from their collections.

Photographs are credited to the person who actually sent that particular photograph. This is not necessarily the same person who "found" or first reported the item. Usually, the illustration you see is the best photograph I have on file of a particular item <u>that did not come from my own collection</u>. Wherever possible, I have used photographs from the collections of others, rather than my own. My name is on the front of this book, and that's enough recognition for me; I would prefer to give credit to others, wherever possible. Unfortunately, this practice elicited the rather disparaging remark that I, the author, am not "a collector." It was a remark that brought laughter from my family, my walls, and the proprietor of my storage bin.

ACKNOWLEDGEMENTS

Although my husband is credited in the dedication of this book, he deserves a word of thanks all his own. No one could be more supportive, understanding and helpful. My children, and now my grandchildren, bravely endure life with a parent who hardly ever has time to bake cookies.

Every "Fox-Hunt" member has contributed to this book. Their enthusiastic sharing of pictures and information is the basis of twelve years of newsletters and two books. Although several "Fox Hunters" have obviously gone far beyond "active membership," I must refrain from naming anyone for fear of leaving someone out or hurting anyone's feelings.

We all owe a special debt of gratitude to the Fox family. During the course of this project, I have had the privilege of knowing all but one of RAF's children, and even several of his grandchildren. They are warm, witty, generous, and absolutely delighted that their father and grandfather is receiving the homage he so richly deserves.

Bettie McKenzie and Fran Woodworth of "The People's Art Project," Red Oak, Iowa, have generously shared information on Fox from their research. They were essential to gaining permission from JII/Sales Promotions Associates, Inc. (formerly The Thos. D. Murphy Co.) to use the Project's slides in this book. Thanks to JII, too, for that permission.

All illustrations credited to the People's Art Project and JII/Sales Promotions Associates, were expertly photographed by HR Studio, Red Oak, Iowa.

Some of the information in the "Publishers" section first appeared in "The Counselor," Advertising Specialty Institute, January, 1979, and Red Wing, Minnesota: Saga of a River Town, by Madeline Angell, published by Dillon Press, 1977. Permission to use information from these sources is gratefully acknowledged.

I would like to Thank Al Wilson, wherever he is, for first suggesting that I contact L-W Book Sales about publishing Book Two.

And last, but certainly not least, thanks to Neil Wood of L-W Book Sales for reprinting Book One, publishing Book Two, and for his patience and expert advice during the preparation of both.

THE PUBLISHERS

The following list of major publishers of works by R. Atkinson Fox appeared on page 37 of Book One:

American Art Works, Coshocton, Ohio
John Baumgarth Co., Chicago
Brown & Bigelow, St. Paul, Minnesota
Louis F. Dow Co.
John Drescher Co., New York
Electro-Tint Engraving Co., Philadelphia
Gerlach Barklow, Joliet,IL.
Edward Gross & Co., New York
Joseph Hoover & Sons, Philadelphia
Ketterlinus, Philadelphia
London Printing & Engraving Co., London, Canada
Master Art Publishers, Chicago
Merchants Publishing Co., Kalamazoo, Michigan
Morris & Bendien, New York
Photo-Chromotype Engraving Co., Philadelphia
The Red Wing Advertising Co.
Southwood Calendars
Edw. Stern & Co., Philadelphia
The Thos. D. Murphy Co., Red Oak, Iowa
K. Wirth

Borin Mfg. Co., Chicago, was inadvertantly omitted from this original list.

Since this list appeared, we have identified more than 50 additional publishers, printers and copyright owners on various prints. Some of them may be abbreviations or sobriquets of the above. They Include:

Allen A. Co., Kenosha, Wis.
American News Co., N.Y.
American Colortype Co., Chicago & N.Y.
American Lithography Co.
Art Interchange Co.
Art publishing Co., Chicago
B.F. Haskin, Chicago
B.P. Co., N.Y.
Beckwith Co., Norwich, Conn.
Bigelow Press, So. Bend, IN
C.D.W. Stern & Co., Phila.
C.E. South
C.E. Perry
C.K. Groves, Phila.
C.R. Gibson & Co.

C.T.W. Co.
Campbell Art Co.
Chapman Co., Brooklyn, N.Y.
Chas. Ehler, Cin.
Chs. Williams, N.Y.
Dalton Press, Manson, Ia.
E.C. Cutler
E.N.
F.A. Schneider (F.A.S.)
Frederickson Co., Chicago
Grit, Williamsport, Pa.
H. McCauley
H. Kenyon
H.L. Young
H.P.W.
Hayes Litho Co., Buffalo, N.Y.
International Harvester Co.
J.W. Crane
John Palmer Co., Phila.
"K." Co., Inc.
K.T. Co., Cin., Ohio
L.C. Co.
Lutz & Gould Co., Burlington, Ia.
M.P. (I think this is Merchants Printing Co.)
O.H.K.
Osborne Co., Newark, N.J. & Toronto
P.D. Thomas, Phila.
R. Hill
R.E. Maskin, Chicago
Seneca Press Publishing Co., Seneca Falls, N.Y.
Souvenir Art Co.
Sparrell Print, Boston
Times Pub. Co., St. Cloud, MN.
Warren Paper Products, Lafayette, IN.
Wilson Chemical Co., Tyrone, Pa.

There may be others that I have missed. This list is provided in the hope that it might be of use to curious collectors and potential researchers who may live near one of these former publishers. Who knows when a name might ring a bell and that serendipitous "connection" lead to a warehouse of old prints?

The Thos. D. Murphy Co.
The People's Art Project

Since Book One was published, a few enterprising individuals have provided useful and interesting information on several of the publishers. Among them is the "dynamic duo" of Bettie McKenzie and Fran Woodworth of Red Oak, Iowa. They are the force behind an enterprise known as "The People's Art Project." (Naturally, they would be the first to protest that many others are involved and deserve credit as well.)

The People's Art Project is the result of a cooperative effort between the Red Oak Library and the Montgomery County Historical Society to celebrate 100 years of calendars produced by the Thos. D. Murphy Co. in Red Oak. Fran Woodworth is the Red Oak librarian; Bettie McKenzie's husband worked for Thos. D. Murphy Co. for 37 years. Bettie is the Project's director.

The first step in the Project's development involved photographing and cataloging more than six thousand calendars from the TDM company archives. This required some degree of cooperation on the part of the company itself, and it provides me with the opportunity to say a word in defense of these calendar companies.

Bettie McKenzie, Project director for The People's Art Project, addressed the 1990 Fox Convention in Cedar Falls, Iowa. Photo by Ben Ross	Fran Woodworth, Red Oak librarian, spoke to the 1991 Fox Covention in Sacramento, CA. Photo by Ben Ross

Fig. 1	Fig. 2

"Washington Thrift Series," a group of monthly mailing cards produced by The Thos. D. Murphy Co. for 1926. Three Featured scenes painted by R. A. Fox: "Washington the Soldier"; "Washington the Surveyor"; and "Washington at Valley Forge." Courtesy People's Art Project & JII/Sales Promotion Associates.

Cover of "The People's Art" exhibit catalog. Photo by author.

Fig. 3

Fig. 4

It is frustrating for researchers, like myself, to know that these few companies that are still in business--Thos. D. Murphy, Brown & Bigelow, Hoover, for example-- have been producing the very treasures we lust after for a century or more and own all this wealth of history and information locked up tightly in their archives. We want to claw at their doors, shouting "Let me in!" In all fairness, however, these companies are private enterprises--not public libraries. They are in business, filling needs and providing jobs. Difficult as it is to accept, even as I say it, these firms have no obligation to researchers and collectors. Those who do open their archives, as The Thos. D. Murphy Co. did, deserve a big public-relations pat on the back.

The intended result of the Project's collection of slides, research notes, interviews and records is a catalog of artists whose works were published by Thos. D. Murphy Co. It will be a gold mine for researchers in a number of areas including art, printing, advertising, history and sociology. Art imitates life, we are told, so the pictures that appear on calendars reflect the culture of the time in which they appeared.

Currently, the only way to examine any of the slides in the Project's collection is to travel to Red Oak. However, efforts are being made to obtain a grant to duplicate the slides so they might be made available, in limitied quantities and for research purposes only, through inter-library loan.

In addition to their initial task of documenting the TDM Co. archives, The People's Art Project developed a traveling exhibit of eighty calendars titled, appropriately, "The People's Art, 1889-1989." The calendars were selected to exemplify the various calendar styles as well as the art that appeared on them. They were selected before anyone associated with the Project had any awareness of "Fox Hunt" or the faithful following that RAF enjoys today. Still, of the eighty calendars traveling with the exhibit, four carry images painted by R. Atkinson Fox--more than any other artist represented. Among those "other" artists, by the way, are Thomas Moran, Maxfield Parrish, Charles Russell, Frederick Remington, Rolf Armstrong and Lynn Bogue Hunt. The beautiful redhead in Jennie Brownscombe's "Breath of Spring" graces the exhibit catalog's cover.

Once Bettie and Fran became aware of "Fox Hunt," they put together a video of the more than eighty slides of works by RAF in the Project's collection. The video, titled "The Fox Hunt"; a catalog of the exhibit, "The People's Art, 1889-1989"; and the catalog of the "People's Art Project" are all available by contacting the Red Oak Public Library.

A Brief Background of Calendar Publishing

Thanks to the efforts of Bettie McKenzie and Fran Woodworth, we also know more about the history of some of the calendar companies than we did before. And The Thos. D. Murphy Co. may very well deserve credit for starting the whole thing.

After the death of Jessie's father in 1887, Edmund and Jessie Osborne moved to Red Oak, Iowa, where Edmund tried to salvage his father-in-law's nearly defunct newspaper, "The Independent." He invited Thomas D. Murphy, a friend from college, to join him.

While the two partners were struggling to keep afloat, Osborne became fascinated with a beautiful watercolor of the proposed new Montgomery County Courthouse. "The atmosphere of Iowa wasn't 'arty' in 1888," he explained later. "At that time I had never seen an even moderately good original painting." Always the entrepreneur, he searched for a way to combine the artwork with local pride in the new courthouse and come up with a profit. Finally the idea came. Osborne & Murphy printed the courthouse picture on cardboard, sold advertising space around the picture and attached a calendar pad. Whether this marked the birth of the art calendar is debatable. (Actually, Ketterlinus Lithographic in Philadelphia may have printed calendars with advertising--but not art--as early as 1850.) However, there can be little doubt that the combination of art and calendars was an innovation for Osborne and Murphy. They believed their idea was original.

By 1895, the Osborne & Murphy Co. was one of the largest manufacturers of art calendars in the United States with customers across the country. Throughout their partnership, Osborne had been the salesman, the entrepreneur, the risk-taker; Murphy was the manufacturer, the practical businessman. Although they remained friends, the time came for them to go their separate ways. Murphy sold his interest in the calendar company to Osborne, agreeing to a five-year non-competition clause. Osborne moved his business to Newark, N.J., expanding all the time.

When Murphy's non-competition clause expired in 1900, he added calendars to his newspaper-publishing business and The Thos. D. Murphy Co. was born. William Cochrane joined the company to develop its sales force. The following preface introduced the 1903 catalog. It is a fascinating lesson in turn-of-the century business. Musson is mentioned but not Fox.

A Few Words Introductory

It is the theory of the Thos D. Murphy Co. that the business concern that does not progress is bound to go the other way. There is not much chance for a standstill, and besides, he would be a very poor business man who would be satisfied with a "standstill" state of affairs. Hence we aim that every year shall show a substantial gain and so far we have not been dissappointed. In 1900 we filled less than 3,000 orders, for 1901 we filled more than 6,000 and the indications are for 1902 that we shall at least pass the 10,000 mark.

This showing has not been attained without effort and expense on our part. In 1901 our line of calendars was a very modest one, indeed, and cost comparatively a small sum to prepare. Our 1902 line was a great step in advance, the pictures and color plates costing much more money. Our 1903 line, however, is such an advance that it hardly admits of comparison with either of its predecessors. One picture alone in this splendid collection cost nearly as much as the entire line of paintings of the previous years.

It is distinctively an art line, the best American and foreign painters contributing for its subjects--you may not be an art critic but you can not fail to recognize the names of some of the artists whose works we have reproduced. Of Americans: HENRY P. SMITH, of Old England Homestead fame; PERCY AND LEON MORAN, in their quaint representation of life in the colonies; ADA L. STEWART, the animal painter; HARRY ROSELAND, whose quaint negro studies are the despair of imitators; E.L. PAXSON, whose delineation of the far west is creating a sensation; MUSS-ARNOLT, foremost painter of dogs, whose work is represented by two notable examples; GEO. HOWELL GAY, whose picture, "A November Day in Old Virginia," is the most sensational success we have ever offered; NIEL MITCHEL, famed for moonlight seas; BRYSON, America's leader in pastelle; MUSSON, who has caught the spirit of the American farm as few others have done; FERRIS, HARTSON, IHLEFELD, BAUER, and others well known in American art. Of Foreigners: ALBERT LYNCH, salon exhibitor and recipient Mediaile de Honeur; GEO. BERNIER, next to Rosa Bonheur, the greatest painter of the draft horse; MASSINI AND PERRIGO, chief in delineation of humorous monkish themes; INNOCENTI, whose sensational coloring we have wonderfully reproduced; BROCK, a master of humorous fox hunting scenes; PAPPERITZ, court painter to the King of Denmark, winner of medal at the World's Fair at Chicago in 1893; VAN SLUYS, pupil of the great Ver Boeckhaven, whom he promises to equal or surpass as a painter of sheep studies; WILMS, whose lifelike pictures of English stag hunting have been immensely popular; VAN ANTRO, MAES, GERETTON, SCHOLER and others well known to everyone familiar with art.

The originals by all of these artists are owned by us--are copyrighted by us and controlled by us. We do not sell jobbers, we do not sell printers, we do not sell anyone but the consumer, and when we have sold him we do not sell the same thing to his neighbor across the way. You only get the best there is, but you alone get it if you buy of us. Don't confuse us with someone else. There is only one calendar manufactory in Red Oak, Iowa, and the famous Red Oak line--known from Maine to California--is ours alone. It is manifest from our reputation and our record that you take no chances in buying of us. We sold goods last season in every state in the Union and in many foreign lands, and a universally satisfied customer was the rule.

Our facilities for the present season have been greatly enlarged in view of the increase in business, which we can reasonably expect, and we are prepared to take care of your orders in a prompt and satisfactory manner. Use the enclosed blank and envelope in ordering and you will be sure of the best goods offered anywhere, and that your order will be executed with painstaking precision.

The Thos. D. Murphy Company

Red Oak, Iowa

(SIC)

By 1904, the TDM Co. had expanded three times and opened a sales branch in England. After undergoing a sale and a merger in the 1980's, the company is known today as JII/Sales Promotion Associates.

"See America First" Series

Reproduced by perfected Tinto Gravure process from the original paintings by R. Addington Fox. Copyright 1918, by Brown & Bigelow, St. Paul, Minn., and Soo, Ontario.

The two great English-speaking nations of America are just becoming acquainted with our own unconquerable resources. Sectionalism is being dissipated by a growing understanding of the essential unity of our geographically distant millions. And with this awakening is coming a more universal realization that from the standpoint of variety and grandeur, America is scenically without a peer. Within our vast limits marked by the Statue of Liberty and the Golden Gate is Nature's playground, resplendent with mighty cataracts and the awesome majesty of lofty, snow-clad peaks. This card is the advance guard of a series, all equally beautiful reproductions of the most noted scenic wonders on the continent each of us is so proud to call "my own, my native land." And as you travel with us to these far corners of America together, we trust that a growing friendship will be strengthened to a point where you will always look to us when you require our kind of sincere service.

Fig. 6

This blurb accompanied the first card in Brown & Bigelow's "See America First" series of monthly mailing cards. Note the spelling--"R. Addington Fox."

Gerlach-Barklow is represented here by this uncut print sheet--absolutely gorgeous in color! 47 x 35. Courtesy Margene & Terry Petros.

Fig. 7

In 1902, Osborne formed a new company, American Colortype Co., specifically for the purpose of commercial letterpress printing. (On several of the TDM Co. Painting Records illustrated in Book One, we find that the American Colortype Co. sometimes produced prints of TDM's Fox paintings.) By 1914, The Osborne Co. had plants in London, Toronto, and Sidney, Australia. Brookwood, the Osborne's new home in Montclair, N.J., was featured in the March, 1913, issue of American Homes and Gardens. Prosperity enabled Osborne to pursue a lifetime love--politics. In 1916, he was elected to the New Jersey State Senate; he died of a heart attack in 1917.

The Osborne-Murphy story serves as a background for several other names today's calendar collectors will recognize. Both Brown & Bigelow and Gerlach-Barklow companies were established by former salesmen of Osborne and Murphy. Others, such as The American Art Works in Coshocton, Ohio, and The Red Wing Advertising Company in Red Wing, Minnesota, were--like Osborne & Murphy--newspaper publishers who gradually added specialty advertising, including art calendars.

Like any idea whose time has come, the successful marriage of art and calendars spread quickly across the country. The Kemper-Thomas Co. started out as printers of wrapping paper. In 1906, a new owner turned the the company's emphasis toward art calendars. Joseph Hoover & Sons had been in the lithography business since 1856. In 1910, they jumped on the calendar bandwagon with a different twist-- blank stock with calendar pads that they sold to local printers. John Baumgarth started a lithography business in Chicago, where he became friends with one of the artists he published, R. Atkinson Fox. By the late 20's, Baumgarth had expanded to South Bend, Indiana. When he went bankrupt in the stock market crash, his South Bend plant was taken over by Brown & Bigelow and renamed The Bigelow Press.

Fox prints #485 through #496 were found in a folio of monthly mailing cards published by the Baumgarth Co., South Bend, Indiana, titled "Touring America's Wonderlands." These pieces appeared on the back of the folio. Courtesy Duane & Dolores Ramsey.

TOURING AMERICA'S WONDERLANDS

True-to-Life reproductions in actual colors by Photo process from original paintings in oil by the eminent artist, R. A. Fox

WE ARE going to take you on an imaginary tour along the highways that lead through Nature's masterpieces of beauty; to rejoice in a visit to the most beautiful of America's vistas of natural splendor, from the cloud-misted snow cap of famous Mount Ranier, through the glories of Yellowstone National Park, and on to the placid glories of the historic Palisades of the Hudson.

We hope this picture series—Touring America's Wonderlands, one of which will be sent you periodically, will prove fully enjoyable.

Please Mail This Back to Us

TOURING AMERICA'S WONDERLANDS

Picture No.

1. 134—Mt. Ranier
2. 135—Mt. Shasta
3. 136—Yosemite Falls
4. 137—Mirror Lake
5. 138—Grand Canyon
6. 139—Lower Falls
7. 140—Pike's Peak
8. 141—Glacier National Park
9. 142—Lookout Mountain
10. 143—The Dells
11. 144—Thousand Islands
12. 145—Palisades of the Hudson

Fox #445, "Where Peace Abides" was also in the Baumgarth "Touring America's Wonderlands" folio, along with the following comments:

Where Peace Abides
From an original oil painting by R. Atkinson Fox.

Mr. Fox has a national reputation for portraying Nature's best on the canvas. This subject truly portrays peace, restfulness, and the beauty of Nature.

It is refreshing, inspiring and encouraging to forget the cares of the day, and reflect with this portrayal of Nature's best.

The picture itself has all the elements of a perfection: namely, wooded countryside, distant hills, sky and water.

We can just imagine ourselves transplanted to such a scene, where we would enjoy the beauty of the entire setting--"Where Peace Abides."

This reproduction will live on the wall of any home or office, because it reflects all that the word "Peace" means.

Fig. 9

This is one of four salesman's sample sets found under the title "The new Stratford Art Calendar Offering." Each set shows a calendar (as in top, left), and four alternative prints that could be ordered for this calendar style. The prints illustrated were 9 1/2 x 7; the overall calendar dimensions were 16 1/4 x 10 1/4. From top left, this portfolio shows two unknown prints; at top right is Wainwright's "The House by the Side of the Road"; at bottom left is RAF's "Off Treasure Island" (Fig. 167, Book One); and Dupre's "The Chieftain's Pride" is at bottom right. The portfolios were published by the John Baumgarth Co. Courtesy Duane & Dolores Ramsey.

Fig. 10
The cover of one of Baumgarth Co.'s "Stratford" portfolios. courtesy Nick Morin.

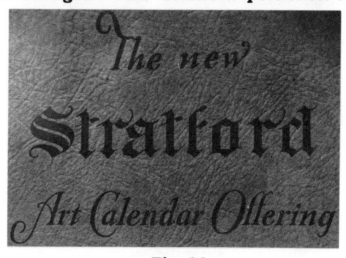

Fig. 11

Several copies of Brown & Bigelow's in-house sales magazine, "The Business Builder," have been found with items of particular interest to Fox collectors. The January 5, 1927 issue, for example, offers a list of "Choice Oil Paintings For Sale" with the following text:

Here are a few choice original paintings from the 1928 Calendar Line. In selling original paintings, Brown & Bigelow retain all advertising and copyright privileges, selling the picture only. As we sell these pictures at very attractive price reductions it is a rare opportunity to secure fine original paintings. All the pictures are framed artistically. Refer to the Bible edition of your Business Builder for facts about the pictures and the artists.

Among the paintings listed are two by R.A.Fox: "The Land of Dreams," Oil, 26 x 35, and "The Good Ship Adventure," Oil, 24 x 30. Each was offered at $300. Subsequent text also explained that "a few original paintings from previous lines" remained to be sold. It was clear that the company expected these paintings to be sold to customers, not salesmen.

In the February 2, 1932, issue of "The Business Builder," however, the salesman got their chance. Six original oil paintings were offered as premiums to the top "Metropolitan" and "Territorial" salesmen of "Anniversary Week." Among the six oil paintings offered were "Indian Girl by R. Atkinson Fox, Original Oil, 27 x 33" ("White Feather," Fig 279, Book One), and two RAF landscapes that we apparently have not found yet.

The Feb. 2, 1927, issue of Brown & Bigelow's "The Business Builder" introduced a new set of mailing cards, the "Dreamland" series. It also provided a bit of information about the artist:

Feb. 2, 1927   *The Business Builder*   13

AND--

The Landscape Series of a Decade

DREAMLAND
Mailing Cards
BY R. ATKINSON FOX

(Painter of "Good Ship Adventure," "Garden of Contentment," "Land of Dreams")

The skill of R. Atkinson Fox as a colorist and the popularity his pictures enjoy are attested by the fact that there are more reproductions of his work than any other living artist.

Fox was born in Toronto, Canada, in 1860. He has studied and traveled extensively in Europe and has exhibited his paintings in the New York Academy and the Art Club of Philadelphia. In his younger days he specialized in portraits, numbering President Cleveland and Sir John MacDonald among the notables who sat for him. President Harrison and Princess Louise of England both had paintings done by Mr. Fox.

R. ATKINSON FOX

CREATOR OF TWO OF FASTEST SELLING 1928 CALENDARS PAINTS NEW MAILING CARD SERIES

All the rich coloring, beautiful light and shadow effects, gorgeous foliage, and deep blues which are making "The Good Ship Adventure" and "The Land of Dreams" two of the best selling Calendars in this year's line, are present in the twelve wonderful subjects which R. Atkinson Fox has just painted for us—the "Dreamland" Mailing Cards.

Throughout this series, Fox has done what so few artists can successfully accomplish—combined the utmost richness of coloring in pleasing pictures that strike a popular chord, and still kept them artistic and beautiful. In such a combination there is great advertising value.

FOX PICTURES ENJOY WIDE-SPREAD POPULARITY

All over the country, art stores are offering prints of Fox pictures at high prices, and everywhere they are "Best Sellers," for this type of picture is exceedingly popular. Once the tremendous salability of Fox Calendar

subjects was firmly established, we lost no time in arranging for a Landscape Series of Mailing Cards which would make this type of picture available to direct mail advertisers. By this time you have received your samples, and as soon as you spread these Cards out and look at them you will see that this series is a real step forward, and that it is direct mail advertising of the finest kind.

DOZENS OF LOGICAL PROSPECTS

Show the DREAMLAND Series to every buyer of Landscape pictures, and don't miss out on this idea—whenever you sell a Fox Calendar order, suggest to your customer that now that he has provided for his publicity advertising, he should also have Direct Mail to maintain constant contact, and that you have a beautiful Mailing Card series that is just the thing for his business, painted by the same artist who painted the Calendar, etc.

The big thing is—DREAMLAND Mailing Cards are certain to be a fast seller—Carry them and show them at least five times a day.

R. C. Stoneman

Fig. 12

16

Of course, as collectors of the works of R. Atkinson Fox, it is the art calendars these companies published that most interest us. We should remember, however, that few of these companies confined their wares to calendars. Many of them put their artworks on puzzles as well as advertising fans and thermometers, further enhancing our collecting. The "monthly mailing calendar" was conceived during the depression, when businesses needed something that wasn't so expensive to mail--something that would fit into a number ten envelope.

In addition, partners in the American Art Works, for example, were the first to bring the process of printing on metal to practical use. The result was the famous Coca-Cola trays. Ketterlinus was known for its W.W.I. "Liberty" posters. One of the partners of the Red Wing Co. is credited with inventing the checkbook cover. The spare-tire cover for automobiles was invented and promoted as an imprinted advertising product by The Southard Co.

The history of these companies is the cultural, social, military, and economic history of our country. There are probably old and/or defunct publishing, printing, and/or advertising companies in your town. You might even find dated histories of these companies in your local library or the archives of a historical society. But a word of caution--delving into such histories can be all-consuming. You might find yourself heading up a Project...or writing a book.

The Red Wing Advertising Company
A Special Find

As mentioned earlier, The Red Wing Advertising Co. was incorporated in 1902, when a group of printers gave up their failing newspaper and turned to advertising. Like so many of these companies, expansion was fast and furious until World War I, the stock market crash and the Depression. By 1932, the company was floating on loans underwritten by a group called "The Santa Claus Club." One of that group was E.S. Hall. By 1937, he was chairman of the board. Josten's acquired the company in 1959.

In 1991, an industrious pair of Fox Hunters in Texas acquired from the daughter of E.S. Hall a very special book. It is a simple, hand-assembled scrapbook with an unassuming, hand-written label on the front that reads "Paintings." It is referred to throughout this text as "the Red Wing Paintings book."

This "Red Wing Paintings book" was apparently a record of the paintings Red Wing bought and made prints of over a period of time. Mr. Hall's daughter believes the handwriting in the book is that of her father. The book contains 159 prints, each with a caption indicating the medium of the original (e.g. "Oil"), its size, title, artist and a dollar amount. The possibility exists that this book was assembled as a catalog of paintings Red Wing was willing to sell; but for our purposes, we are going to assume that it was a record of paintings purchased and their purchase price. The book contained ten already-listed Fox prints, and thirteen "new finds."

In an interesting sidelight, one of the three printers who originated Red Wing was C.S. Sultzer. Several of the captions in the Paintings book list the artist as "Sultzer." Apparently either C.S. or one of his relatives was an artist.

And in a final note of irony, we learn that after Jostens acquired the advertising company in 1959, they built a new plant in the industrial section of Red Wing. The old plant was demolished in the early 1960's--by a heavy-equipment company owned by Mr. Hall's son-in-law.

A page from the Red Wing "Paintings" book shows an Ingerle (misspelled "<u>E</u>ngerle"), two "Sultzers," and a Fox. Courtesy Margene & Terry Petros.

Fig. 13

OIL PAINTINGS

One of the saddest pieces of information to come out of the research on this project was a copy of a note from the Thos. D. Murphy Co. files. It is titled "Painting Destroyed Per Mr. Cochrane and T.D. Murphy, July 8, 1940." Among the twelve paintings listed is "An Interesting Family--Fox." (Of course, this painting--or at least one with the same title--was marketed with the signature "Musson.") Because so few oils are found, in comparison to the number of prints, one is inclined to think this was not an isolated practice.

A new find among oils is an exciting event. It is always fun to be able to match one up with a listed print. On at least one occasion, we have been able to identify an unsigned print as RAF because the signed oil was found. And oils with no listed prints offer hope that the prints are out there--somewhere.

Naturally, prices for original oil paintings by R. Atkinson Fox are rising steadily. And with increased value comes the increased risk of fraud. We know of at least two instances in which RAF's signature was forged on a painting. If you are contemplating investing a substantial sum of money in a painting, be sure you are buying from a reputable dealer or auctioneer who will stand behind the piece. If possible, ask a paintings curator at a major art museum or gallery to examine the painting and confirm that the signature is as old as the painting.

Of course, if you are like a certain gentleman who found a signed Fox oil in a remote shop in the Adirondacks for $27.00, and you can afford to risk $27.00-- go for it! Other than the one that was given to a collector, this is the lowest price reported. The highest price that has been reported to me was close to $5,000.

No prices or values are provided for the oils illustrated here out of consideration for the owners. Each oil painting should be evaluated and appraised separately, and such an investment should be made only after consultation with an expert.

"Royal Gorge." R. Atkinson Fox. 36 x 26. Courtesy William Bilsland

Fig. 14

Untitled. Oil on board. R.A. Fox. 9 x 11 1/2. Private collection

Fig. 15

Untitled. Oil on canvas. R.A. Fox. 24 x 30. (In pencil on back of canvas is written, #2324.) Private collection.

Fig. 16

"Mount Shasta." R.A. Fox. 40 x 32. (Paper label on back gives title, size, and remarks: "Painted by R.A. Fox.) Courtesy Pat Gibson.

Fig. 17

"In the Heart of the Sierra Nevadas." R.A. Fox. (Oil of #418.) 55 x 38. Photo by author.

William Bilsland, Jr., with his oil of #418, "In the Heart of the Sierra Nevadas." Photo by author.

Fig. 18

Fig. 19

Untitled. R.A. Fox. Courtesy Pat Gibson.

Untitled. Oil on wood. R.A. Fox. 14 x 17. Courtesy Pat Gibson.

Fig. 20

Fig. 21

"October Days." (Oil of Fig. 84, Book I.) R.A. Fox. 32 x 24. Private collection.

Fig. 22

Untitled. (Oil of Fig. 76, Book I. Please note: Captions for Figs. 75 & 76, Book I, are <u>reversed.</u>) Courtesy Ben & Sandra Ross.

Fig. 23

Untitled. R.A. Fox. 24 x 30. Private collection.

Fig. 24

Untitled. Oil on canvas. R.A. Fox. 20 1/2 x 29. Courtesy Donald W. Ross.

Fig. 25

Untitled. R.A. Fox. 8 1/2 x 11 1/4. This looks just like Fig. 25, Book I, but the signatures are different. Courtesy Pat Gibson.

"Sunset in Normandy." (Oil of #559.) R.A. Fox. 33 x 44. Courtesy Pat Gibson.

Fig. 26

Fig. 27

Untitled. R.A. Fox. Oil of #519 on fringed canvas. Courtesy Pat Gibson.

Untitled. Oil on canvas. R.A. Fox. 26 x 38. Courtesy Donald W. Ross.

Fig. 28

Fig. 29

Untitled. (Oil of Fig. 62-M, Book I.) Courtesy Ben & Sandra Ross.

Untitled. R.A. Fox. Courtesy Pat Gibson.

Fig. 30

Fig. 32

Untitled. R.A. Fox. 20 x 30. Courtesy Evelyn Payne

Untitled. R.A. Fox. 24 x 38. (Compare to Figs. 306, 307, and 326, Book I.) Private collection.

Fig. 33

Fig. 34

"In the Brook." R.A. Fox. (Oil of #616.) Private collection.

Fig. 35

Untitled. R.A. Fox. Oil exhibited at David & Sons Fine Arts, Laguna Beach, Ca. Photo courtesy Duane & Dolores Ramsey.

Fig. 36

"When the Day is Done." (Oil of #600.) R.A. Fox. 14 1/2 x 29 1/2. Courtesy Pat Gibson.

Fig. 37

Untitled. R.A. Fox. 35 x 26. Courtesy James & Oral Potere.

Fig. 38

"Blue Lake." (Oil of Fig. 210, Book I.) R.A. Fox. 16 x 22. Courtesy Donald W. Ross.

Untitled. R.A. Fox. A very different subject for Fox. Brings to mind the "humorous monkish themes" by "Massini and Perrigo" mentioned in the introduction to Thos. D. Murphy Co.'s 1903 catalog. 20 x 24. Courtesy Pat Gibson.

Fig. 39

Fig. 40

Untitled. R.A. Fox. 12 x 14. Courtesy Pat Gibson.

Untitled. R.A. Fox. 9 x 10. Courtesy Pat Gibson.

Fig. 41

Fig. 42

John Mazdra displayed his oil of #640, "Repairs of All Kinds," at the 1989 Fox convention in St. Louis. Photo by author.

"Repairs of All Kinds." R.A. Fox. (Oil of #640.) Photo by author.

Fig. 43

Fig. 43-a

"In the Rockies." Oil on board. R.A Fox. 35 x 57 1/2. Courtesy Ben & Sandra Ross.

Ben & Sandra Ross at home with their Fox oil painting, "In the Rockies." Courtesy the owners.

Fig. 44

Fig. 44-a

Untitled. Oil on canvas. R.A. Fox. 20 x 24 1/4. This is different from both Lincoln prints we have listed. Courtesy Margene & Terry Petros.

Untitled. R.A. Fox. 24 x 20. Courtesy Pat Gibson.

Fig. 45

Fig. 46

Untitled. Oil on canvas. R.A. Fox 12 x 18. Courtesy Pat Gibson.

Fig. 47

"Ring Around Rosy." R.A. Fox. (Original of #396.) 18 x 28 1/2. Courtesy Gene Stapleton.

Fig. 48

LANDSCAPES--NO MOUNTAINS

(#382) "Geyser." R.A. Fox. Actually, the only similarity between this & Fig. 151, Book I, is that they both depict "Old Faithful." The backgrounds are completely different, and there are no people in this. 11 x 8. Courtesy Deanna Hulse.

Fig. 49

(#371) Untitled. R.A. Fox. Beautiful scene bathed in golden light. Really different. Setting sun may not show up in black & white. 12 x 24. Courtesy Shaw collection.

Fig. 50

(#561) Untitled. R.A. Fox. A wooden bridge covers a narrow stream meandering through a field of trees in blossom--perhaps an apple orchard? 7 1/2 x 9 1/2. Courtesy Wm. C. & Becky Fox.

Fig. 51

(#343) "The Mystic Hour." R.A. Fox. 11 x 8 1/2. Courtesy Schmidt collection.

Fig. 52

31

(#560) "Moonlight at the Camp." #1174, R.A. Fox. © F.A.S. Night scene. 9 3/4 x 7 3/4. Courtesy Duane & Dolores Ramsey.

Fig. 53

(#368) "The Witching Hour." R.A. Fox. Edward Gross & Co. Trees, stream, & blue sky. 16 x 10. Courtesy Ron & Bernie Shaw.

Fig. 54

(#445) "Where Peace Abides." R.A. Fox. 9 x 7. Also found on a 1934 calendar by "The Bigelow Press," South Bend, IN. Courtesy Pat Gibson.

Fig. 55

(#495) "Thousand Islands." (Baumgarth, T.A.W. #144, R.A. Fox). Small, foliage-covered "islands." 5 1/4 x 3 1/2. Courtesy Duane & Dolores Ramsey.

Fig. 56

(#542) "Sunrise." R.A. Fox. Misty morning view of a stream in grays, greens, yellows, and orange. 12 x 8. Collection Ann Fox Mergenthaler. Photo by author.

Fig. 57

(#475) "Nature's Hidden Places." R.A. Fox. Water in foreground-- huge rocks to either side. 11 1/4 x 8 3/4, 10 x 8. Also found, signed, on advertising fan. Collection Ann Fox Mergenthaler. Photo by author.

Fig. 58

(#477) Untitled. R.A. Fox. 18 x 14. (Also reported with signature, "W. Thompson.") Courtesy Barb Kratz.

Fig. 59

Detail from print with Thompson signature. Courtesy Ben & Sandra Ross.

Fig. 59-a

(#449) "Autumn Glow." R.A. Fox. Print features yellows & browns. 18 x 40. (See Library of Congress listing pg. 141, Book I.) Courtesy Duane & Dolores Ramsey.

(#592) "The Path to Home." No. 458. R.A. Fox. 6 x 8. Courtesy Duane & Dolores Ramsey.

Fig. 60

Fig. 61

(#531) "Nature's Sentinels." R.A. Fox. Tree trunks and creek. 1922 calendar. Print size, 11 x 8. Courtesy Pat Gibson.

Fig. 62

LANDSCAPES--NO WATER

(#608). "Popocatapel--Mexico." R.A. Fox. © 1912, Red Wing Pub. Co., "Famous Scenic Wonders of America," series of monthly mailing cards. May, 1913, adv. calendar. 6 x 4. Ann Fox Mergenthaler collection. Photo by author.

(#604). "Mount Sir Donald--Canada." R.A. Fox. © 1912, Red Wing Pub. Co., Famous Scenic Wonders of America (FSWA) series. March, 1913, adv. calendar. 6 x 4. Courtesy Margene & Terry Petros.

Fig. 63

(#405). "Where Giants Wrought." R.A. Fox. Golden sunlight illuminates this canyon scene. 6 x 4, Courtesy Barb Kratz.

Fig. 65

Fig. 64

36

(#393). "The Canyon." R.A. Fox. Sun-drenched rocks on either side--setting sun in background. Found on a 1915 calendar advertising Calumet baking powder. 9 x 7. Courtesy Jan Bittner.

Fig. 66

(#333). "A Glorious Solitude." R.A Fox. ©. 1915, The American Art Works, Coshocton, Ohio. (Signature on print--all other info. printed below image.) 8 1/2 x 12. Collection Ann Fox Mergenthaler. Photo by author.

Fig. 67

(#387). "The Mountain Trail." R.A. Fox. #1641, published by Wilson Chemical Co., Tyrone, Pa. ©. 1912, by P.O. Thomas, Phila. 14 x 11, 20 x 16. Courtesy Deanna Hulse.

Fig. 68

(#675). Untitled. R.A. Fox. 13 5/16 x 20. Courtesy Hugh Hetzer.

Fig. 69

(#530) "Mount of the Holy Cross-Colorado." R.A. Fox. ©. 1912, by Red Wing Adv. Co., Red Wing, Minn. This view of the mountain is with a 1915 calendar on one of the "Famous Scenic Wonders of America" series of monthly mailing cards in size 6 x 4. It has also been found on a 1913 calendar that is a postcard. Image size is 3 x 2 1/2. Postcard 3 1/2 x 5 1/2. Courtesy Margene & Terry Petros.

(#476). "The Majesty of Nature." R.A. Fox. 8 x 11. Collection Ann Fox Mergenthaler. Photo by author.

Fig. 71

(#524). "Mount Rainier." ©. 1913, Red Wing Adv. Co. R.A. Fox. 6 x 4, 16 x 10 1/2. Courtesy Pat Gibson.

Fig. 72

Fig. 70

(#523). Untitled. R.A. Fox. 9 x 7. Courtesy Duane & Dolores Ramsey.

(#413). "Mountain Glow." R.A. Fox. 6 x 5. Courtesy Donna Robinson.

Fig. 73

Fig. 74

(#351). "The Snow-Capped Peaks." R.A. Fox. With a sprinkling of wildflowers and a winding path, we see a softening of the rugged canyon scene. 11 x 8. Courtesy John & Darlene Boland.

(#331). "The Rosy Glow of the Land of Promise." R.A. Fox. The "Rosy Glow" is the sunset reflected on the mountains at right. 8 1/2 x 6 1/2. Also found in 13 x 10 on a 1927 calendar. Courtesy Nick Morin.

Fig. 75

Fig. 76

(#611). "Pike's Peak from Garden of the Gods." "Signed." 17 1/2 x 24 1/2. Courtesy Duane & Dolores Ramsey

(#674). "End of the Trail." R.A. Fox. DLB 2164. ©. 1927, Brown & Bigelow. Found on a blotter advertising Brown & Bigelow's products and services. 3 3/8 x 6 1/8. Courtesy Ben & Sandra Ross.

Fig. 77

Fig. 78

An enlarged view of "End of the Trail." Ross.

Fig. 78-a

(#457). Untitled, #3616. R.A. Fox. This has also been found, with the same stock number (3616), with the following printed on the back: "This Picture Can Only Be Used on the \ Home Sweet Home, Golden Swan, Economy Semi-DeLuxe, Basket Weave, and the Standard Exclusive Calendars. Courtesy Keith & Linda Bettis.

Fig. 79

(#330). "The Magic Forest." R.A. Fox. With its deep browns, delicate pastels and smoky blue mountains, this does indeed look like an enchanted land. 12 x 9, 16 x 12. Courtsey Loretta Goad.

Fig. 80

LANSCAPES--WITH MOUNTAINS AND WATER

(#402). "Lake Louise-Alberta." R.A. Fox. There are lists of freight and passenger representatives on the back, so this print may have been part of a railroad poster. 11 x 14. Courtesy Pat Gibson.

(#551). Untitled. R.A. Fox. ©. 1912 by P.D. Thomas, Phila. The signature at left has been cut off to reveal only...son Fox. However, the white margin was visible at left, so it was trimmed before printing. 11 x 14. Courtesy Ben & Sandra Ross.

Fig. 81

Fig. 82

(#658). "Colorado Canyon." R.A. Fox. ©. H.L. Young. Print is 3 x 2 1/4. Courtsey Pat Gibson.

(#590). "Solitary Heights." R.A. Fox. Courtesy Mary & Len Henning.

Fig. 83

Fig. 84

43

(#424). Untitled. R.A. Fox. 10 x 7 1/2. Courtesy Barb Kratz.

Fig. 85

(#525). "Mount LeFroy." R.A. Fox. The Dalton Press, Manson, Ia. "Mount LeFroy is one of the loftiest & most beautiful mountains in Canada." 4 x 3 1/2 on 1916 calendar. Courtesy Pat Gibson.

Fig. 86

(#409). "Columbia River--Oregon." John Drescher Co., Inc. This print is not signed, but the title and publisher match the Library of Congress list. 14 x 20. Courtesy Barb Kratz.

Fig. 87

(#659). "A New England Coast." Attributed to R.A. Fox in Thos. D. Murphy catalog. A ship is visible on the far left horizon. Courtesy Margene & Terry Petros.

Fig. 88

44

(#448). Untitled. R.A. Fox. 12 x 22. Courtesy Barb Kratz.

(#372). Untitled. R.A. Fox. 1925 calendar. 14 x 28. Courtesy Louise Mendyk.

Fig. 89

Fig. 90

(#358). "Heart of the Seilkerts." R.A. Fox. 1927 calendar. 6 x 4. Courtesy Mary Battaglia.

(#732). "On the Way to the Mill." Attributed to RAF in Red Wing Paintings Book. Oil was listed at 24 x 30 and $19.50! Print is 6 x 9. Shown here on a 1928 Red Wing calendar. Courtesy Margene & Terry Petros.

Fig. 91

Fig. 92

(#606). "Clear Creek Canyon--Colorado." R.A. Fox. Red Wing Pub. Co., Famous Scenic Wonders of America series of monthly mailing cards. Nov., 1913, adv. calendar. 6 x 4. Courtesy Margene & Terry Petros.

(#661). "The Winding River." R.A. Fox. © 1920, The American Art Works, Coshocton, Ohio. Print is 2 x 3 1/2 on a 4 x 9 blotter. Courtesy Pat Gibson.

Fig. 94

(#508). Untitled. R.A. Fox. 6 x 8, 9 1/2 x 12 1/2. Courtesy Pat Gibson.

Fig. 93

Fig. 95

(#416). "The Snow-capped Mountain." R.A. Fox. 3 x 2 1/2, 10 x 8, 17 x 14. Also found on an advertising fan. Courtesy Loretta Goad.

(#377). "Mount Lindbergh." Signed. Notice the airplane at top right. 16 x 10. Found on a 1925 Calendar by Donna Robinson.

Fig. 96

Fig. 97

(#423). "The Home of the West Wind." R.A. Fox. © Souvenir Art Co. 7 1/4 x 10, 14 x 23. Courtesy Barb Kratz.

(#332). "At the Foot Hills of Pike's Peak." R.A. Fox. 9 x 7. Courtesy Deanna Hulse.

Fig. 98

Fig. 99

(#324). "Mt. Rainier Glowing in Rosy Splendor." Painting by R.A. Fox. The K.T. Co., Cin., Ohio. found on a 1924 calendar. 13 1/2 x 16. Courtesy Loretta Goad.

(#593). "A Fairy-Like Vision: Mount Shasta in the Sky." Painting by R.A. Fox. Mt. Shasta, bathed in a golden glow, provides the "vision." 16 x 22. Courtesy Duane & Dolores Ramsey.

Fig. 100

Fig. 101

(#391). "Mid Mountain Verdure." R.A. Fox. © C.E. Perry. 8 x 6. Courtesy Pat Gibson.

(#591). "Guardian of the Valley." Reproduced from original oil painting by R.A. Fox. © Louis F. Dow Co., St. Paul. 8 1/4 x 11 1/4. Also found, titled, as a 250 pc., interlocking "Perfect Picture Puzzle, No. 1410," 13 1/2 x 10. Just the center mid-to-bkgrnd of this print has also been found on an unmarked puzzle. This photo courtesy Pat Gibson.

Fig. 102

Fig. 103

Just the center background of "Guardian of the Valley" on an unmarked puzzle. Courtesy Ben & Sandra Ross.

"Guardian of the Valley," complete on a "Perfect Picture Puzzle, No. 1410," 13 1/2 x 10. Courtesy Ben & Sandra Ross.

Fig. 103-a

Fig. 103-b

"Guardian of the Valley," puzzle box. Courtesy Ben & Sandra Ross.

(#535). "Mountain Lake." R.A. Fox. John Drescher Co., Inc., N.Y. Colors are mostly gray and rust. 20 x 40. Courtesy Mikel McAllister.

Fig. 103-c

Fig. 104

49

(#733). "Purple Majesty." Attributed to RAF in Red Wing Paintings Book. Here you can see the notations below the 6 x 9 print. The oil is listed at 32 1/2 x 23 3/4 and $200. This has also been found on an 8 x 12 1/2 (trimmed) unsigned, 1930 calendar sample and a 9 x 14 (complete) unsigned print. Courtesy Margene & Terry Petros.

(#568) "Pure and Healthful." R.A. Fox. (See oil, Fig. 25-top, Book I.) 7 1/2 x 10 1/2. Courtesy Pat Gibson.

Fig. 105

Fig. 106

(#570). "A Golden Sunset." R.A. Fox. 7 x 9 1/2. Courtesy Loren Johnson.

(#660). "Birch Bordered Waters." R.A. Fox. The signature is indistinct, I am told, and blends with the brown & tan tones at lower right. 16 x 10, 10 x 6 1/2. Courtesy Margene & Terry Petros.

Fig. 107

Fig. 108

(#422). "Sunland." R.A. Fox. A number of "portions" in various sizes have been found. One carries a 1927 copyright by the Master Arts Publishers. Some examples extend a little farther to the right (but don't show all of the left side.) Most sizes are within an inch of 14 x 22. This photo courtesy Loretta Goad.

Fig. 109

(#541). "Where Peace Abides." (Also titled "The Heart of the Hills.") R.A. Fox. 10 x 7. Also found on a 6 x 4 cardboard plaque with red flowers & "God Is Love" written in calligraphy; and in a book called "Paths of Uprightness," ©. 1933, by Metropolitan Church Association. This photo courtesy Barbara Kern.

Fig. 110

"Where Peace Abides" on a 6 x 4 cardboard plaque. Courtesy Barb Kratz.

Fig. 110-a

(#390). "Nature's Grandeur." R.A. Fox. ©. C.E. South, St. Louis, 1930. Found on a 1932 calendar. 6 x 8. Courtesy Pat Gibson.

Fig. 111

(#438). "Paradise Bay." R.A. Fox. ©. 1927, Brown & Bigelow, St. Paul, Minn. Majestic America Series, mailing card with calendar. Courtesy Barbara Kern.

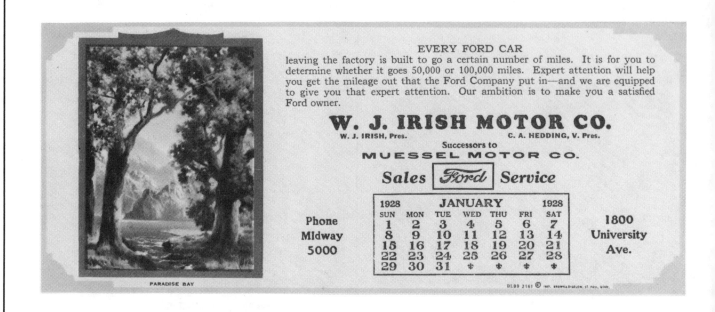

Fig. 112

(#439). "When Evening Shadows Fall." R.A. Fox. Majestic America Series, mailing card with calendar. Courtesy Barbara Kern.

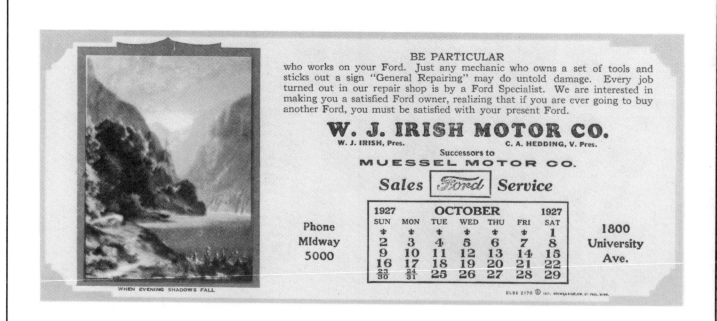

Fig. 113

(#440) "Mountain Majesty." R.A. Fox. Majestic America series, mailing card with calendar. Courtesy Barbara Kern. Note: Barbara Kern has a set of these mailing cards including Jan., Feb., Mar., Aug., Oct., Nov., and Dec. February's picture is #259 (Fig. 91, Book I), "Grandeurs of Nature"; March is #308 (Fig. 135, Book I), "Heart of the Hills"; Jan., Oct., and Nov., are #438, #439, And #440 (described above), and Feb., Mar., Aug., and Nov. are unsigned. However, from the description below, we can presume they are by Fox. A note included with the January card reads as follows: "Reproduced by perfected Off-set process from the original paintings by R.A. Fox. Copyright 1919, by Brown & Bigelow, St. Paul, Minn. and Sault Ste. Marie, Ont. / As vague hearsay in regard to the scenic beauties of the Old World is giving way before the first hand knowledge of our valiant soldiers Overseas, we have deeper appreciation for the scenic value of our own land. We have gained a new point of view of our dooryard. The unusual in topography attracts tourists, vivid descriptions are printed of them and their fame is a household by-word. But this series of twelve mailing cards of which this is the first, depicts graphically the meadow lands, hills, lakes and running water of our own vast land--beautiful bits which everyone of us know by heart and enjoy from the rising to the setting of the sun every day. / As these scenes remind us of the beauty that lies around about us, we trust that our message upon these cards will find an audience, for we have firm desire to be of service to you."

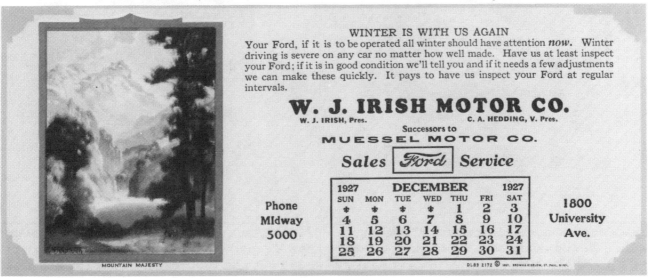

Fig. 114

(#506). "Just Before Sunrise." (R.A. Fox, ©. 1919, Brown & Bigelow.) "Majestic America" series of monthly mailing cards. Also found as a 10 x 8 print, © 1928 by Brown & Bigelow. Courtesy Barbara Kern.

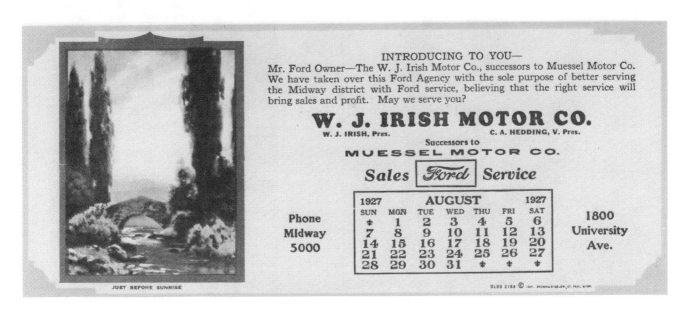

Fig. 115

(#485). "Mount Rainier." (Baumgarth, "Touring America's Wonderlands" [T.A.W] #134, R.A. Fox). 5 1/4 x 3 1/2. Courtesy Duane & Dolores Ramsey.

Fig. 116

(#486). "Mount Shasta." (Baumgarth, "Touring America's Wonderlands" [T.A.W.] #135, R.A. Fox). 5 1/4 x 3 1/2. Courtesy Duane & Dolores Ramsey.

Fig. 117

(#489). "Grand Canyon." (Baumgarth, "Touring America's Wonderlands" [T.A.W.] #138, R.A. Fox). 5 1/4 x 3 1/2. Courtesy Duane & Dolores Ramsey.

Fig. 118

(#491) "Pike's Peak." (Baumgarth, "Touring America's Wonderlands" [T.A.W.] #140, R.A. Fox). 5 1/4 x 3 1/2. Courtesy Duane & Dolores Ramsey.

Fig. 119

(#492). "Glacier Nat'l Park." (Baumgarth, "Touring America's Wonderlands" {T.A.W.} #141, R.A. Fox). 5 1/4 x 3 1/2. Courtesy Duane & Dolores Ramsey.

Fig. 120

(#488). "Mirror Lake" (Baumgarth, [T.A.W.] #137, R.A. Fox). 5 1/4 x 3 1/2. Courtesy Duane & Dolores Ramsey

Fig. 121

(#493) "Lookout Mountain." (Baumgarth, "Touring America's Wonderlands" series of monthly mailing cards. [T.A.W.] #142, R.A. Fox). 5 1/4 x 3 1/2. Courtesy Duane & Dolores Ramsey.

Fig. 122

(#494) "The Dells of Wisconsin." (Baumgarth, "Touring America's Wonderlands" [T.A.W.] #143, R.A. Fox). 5 1/4 x 3 1/2. Courtesy Duane & Dolores Ramsey.

Fig. 123

(#607). "Mount Shasta--California." R.A. Fox. ©. 1912, Red Wing Adv. Co., "Famous Scenic Wonders of America" series of monthly mailing cards. Found on June, 1913, adv. calendar. 6 x 4. Courtesy Margene & Terry Petros.

(#737). "Land Where the Mountains are Nameless / And the Valley Unpeopled and Still." Painting by R.A. Fox. K.T. Co., Cin., Ohio. 1935 calendar sample. 8 3/4 x 4 3/4. Courtesy Margene & Terry Petros.

Fig. 124

Fig. 125

56

LANDSCAPES WITH WATERFALLS

(#419). "Sentinel of the Ages." Unsigned. This hasn't been found in signed form. However, if you'll compare this print to the info. and picture on pg. 39-40 of Book I, you'll see why there can be no doubt that this is Fox. 16 x 11 1/2. Ann Fox Mergenthaler collection. Photo by author.

Fig. 126

(#418). "In the Heart of the Sierra Nevadas." R.A. Fox. 15 x 10. Courtesy Pat Gibson.

Fig. 127

(#325). Untitled. R.A. Fox. 14 x 11. Courtesy Loretta Goad.

Fig. 128

(#652). "The Great Divide." R.A. Fox. Series 12-2355. ©. 1911, American Art Works, Coshocton, Ohio. 8 1/4 x 12 1/4. Ann Fox Mergenthaler collection. Photo by author.

Fig. 129

(#673). "The Mountain in All Its Glory." R.A. Fox 10 1/2 x 7. Found on a 1914 calendar by Pat Gibson.

(#567). "Golden West." Painting by R.A. Fox. Several Fox Hunters own prints of this landscape that is so similar to others we have listed but is distinguished by a two-tier waterfall in the background. 10 x 8, 13 x 15. Found on a 1934 calendar by Pat Gibson.

Fig. 130

Fig. 131

(#694). Untitled. Sgnd. "R. Atkins..." ("in a manner identical to RAF"). 9 x 13. Courtesy Margene & Terry Petros.

(#487). "Yosemite Falls" (Baumgarth, "Touring America's Wonderlands" [T.A.W.] #136, R.A. Fox). 5 1/4 x 3 1/2. Courtesy Duane & Dolores Ramsey.

Fig. 132

Fig. 133

(#414). "A Shrine of Nature." R.A. Fox. #31116, Chapman Co., Brooklyn, N.Y. Courtesy Donna Robinson.

Fig. 134

(#360). "The Artist Supreme." R.A Fox. Tintagravure, Brown & Bigelow, St. Paul, Minn. Waterfall into a tumbling stream with a rainbow arched across the mist. 10 x 6, 10 x 8. Courtesy Barbara Kern.

Fig. 135

(#490). "Lower Falls--Yellowstone Park" (Baumgarth, "Touring America's Wonderlands" [T.A.W.] #139, R.A. Fox). 5 1/4 x 3 1/2. Courtesy Duane & Dolores Ramsey.

Fig. 136

(#564). "Vernal Falls." R.A. Fox. © M.P. Co. ("Merchant's Publishing Co." is stamped on the back of the print.) 11 x 8. Ann Fox Mergenthaler collection. Photo by author.

Fig. 137

(#605). "Vernal Falls-- Yosemite, California." R.A. Fox. ©. 1912, Red Wing. Pub. Co., "Famous Scenic Wonders of America." (Looks the same as #564, but it _is_ different.) 6 x 4. Courtesy Margene & Terry Petros.

(#366). "Giant Steps Falls, B.C." Untitled. R.A. Fox. 11 1/2 x 8. (WARNING: This print is reproduced--in 9 x 12 & "guaranteed to look old.") Courtesy Ron & Bernie Shaw.

Fig. 138

Fig. 139

SHIPS AND BOATS

(#526). "Sunrise, Coast of Maine." R.A. Fox. The Lutz & Gould Co., Burlington, Ia. No.432, ©. 1901. 4 x 6. Found on a 1902 calendar by Mark & Carol Graham.

(#610). "Kap Nome, Alaska." Efter Maleri av (After painting by) Robert Atkinson Fox. Jul i Vesterheimen, 1936. (Also, "Cape Nome." No. 2039, attributed to R.A. Fox., publisher Red Wing Adv. Co.) 8 x 11. Collection Ann Fox Mergenthaler. Photo by author.

Fig. 140

Fig. 141

(#569). "Cool & Refreshing." R.A. Fox. (See oil, fig. 25, bottom, Book I.) 7 1/2 x 10 1/2. Courtesy Pat Gibson.

(#432). "Cottage By the Sea." 9841. Painting by R.A. Fox. ©. F.A.S. 12 x 10. Courtesy Pat Gibson.

Fig. 142

Fig. 143

63

(#496). "Palisades of the Hudson." (Baumgarth, "Touring America's Wonderlands" series, [T.A.W.] #145, R.A. Fox). 5 1/4 x 3 1/2. Courtesy Duane & Dolores Ramsey.

Fig. 144

(#559). "Sunset in Normandy." R.A. Fox. The print is unsigned & untitled. We are taking the signature and title from the oil painting. 16 x 21. Courtesy Pat Gibson.

Fig. 145

(#361). "The Treasure Fleet." R.A. Fox. Louis F. Dow. This has also been found in a 1940, New Standard Encyclopedia, published in Chicago. Encyclopedia print is marked "©. Louis F. Dow Co." and measures 4 3/8 x 7 3/4. Photo courtesy Clare Cerda. Her print is 8 x 11.

Fig. 146

(#447). "The Heights of Quebec." R.A. Fox. Brown & Bigelow, 1920. "12th in a series of Natural Wonders including Niagra Falls, The Falls of Yellowstone, and the Natural Bridge of Virginia." Calendar print, 6 x 4. Also found, signed, on a blotter. Photo courtesy Pat Gibson.

Fig. 147

(#447). Has also been found titled "The Heights of Quebec, The Gateway to Canada, A Spot of Historical Fame." ©. 1918, Brown & Bigelow, St. Paul, Minn. and So. Ont. 1919 calendar. 10 x 5. Courtesy Nick Morin.

Fig. 148

(#594). "The Port of Heart's Desire." R.A. Fox. ©. Brown & Bigelow Co. 11 x 8. Also found, unsigned, 13 x 6, attached to a 1929 calendar. Courtesy Loren Johnson.

Fig. 150

(#522). "In New York Bay (where liberty stands at the threshold of America)." R.A. Fox. 6 x 4 calendar card. Also found on a signed & titled advertising blotter. Photo courtesy Duane & Dolores Ramsey.

Fig. 149

GARDEN SCENES

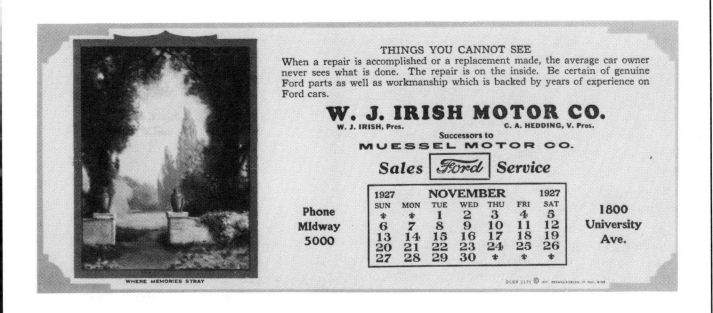

THINGS YOU CANNOT SEE

When a repair is accomplished or a replacement made, the average car owner never sees what is done. The repair is on the inside. Be certain of genuine Ford parts as well as workmanship which is backed by years of experience on Ford cars.

W. J. IRISH MOTOR CO.

W. J. IRISH, Pres.   C. A. HEDDING, V. Pres.

Successors to

MUESSEL MOTOR CO.

Sales *Ford* Service

Phone
Midway
5000

1927	NOVEMBER					1927
SUN	MON	TUE	WED	THU	FRI	SAT
✦	✦	1	2	3	4	5
6	7	8	9	10	11	12
13	14	15	16	17	18	19
20	21	22	23	24	25	26
27	28	29	30	✦	✦	✦

1800
University
Ave.

WHERE MEMORIES STRAY

Fig. 151

(#329). "Dreamy Paradise." Signed "Fox." 16 x 12. Also found on an unsigned puzzle, 10 1/2 x 14 1/2, titled "Paradise." Courtesy Loretta Goad.

We don't normally accept a signature of "Fox" as ample proof that the image was created by RAF. The following was found on the back of one example of #329. Courtesy Pat Gibson.

Dreamy Paradise
Where the air is always cool and refreshing. Where the clouds are fleecy white and lazily float across the sky. Where the flowers, the trees, the grass, and the mountains join in with the universal harmony of nature. Where everything is as it should be and nothing is lacking to assure complete happiness-that's Dreamy Paradise. You yourself know what kind of a place you would want "Dreamy Paradise" to be. Devoid of cares and troubles, of dust and grime and worry. In short, a paradise, an ideal, dreamy paradise. No artist equals R.A. Fox in his ability to create picturefairylands. More reproductions of his works have been made than of those of any other living artist. Many prints of his paintings command fancy prices at art stores. We are glad to offer you this reproduction of one of his finest on our art calendar.

Fig. 152

Fig. 152-a

(#678). Untitled. R.A. Fox. ©. 1926, Manz-Chicago. 12 x 16. A reversed or "mirror" image has also been found. Courtesy Shirley Timm.

(#679). "Garden Gate." R.A. Fox (printed in bottom margin). (This information comes from two prints-- one with the title & no artist info. & the other with the artist attribution & no title.) 16 x 12. This photo courtesy Loren Johnson.

Fig. 153

Fig. 154

(#518). "In a Lovely Garden/Where Dreams Come True." (Compare to #10, [Fig. 185, Book I], "Promenade.") You might not be able to see the log cabin, barely visible through the gate at left. 9 x 12, 16 x 20. Courtesy Duane & Dolores Ramsey.

Fig. 155

The following appears on the back of #518.
"From an original painting by R.A. Fox. Copyright by the Kemper-Thomas Co., Cincinnati, Ohio./ And the Lord God planted a garden eastward in Eden;/And out of the ground made the Lord God to grow every tree that is pleasant to the sight;/And a river went out of Eden to water the garden./ Genesis ii; 8, 9, 10.'/ Painters, and writers of Romance, ever since the days described in Holy Writ, have found a theme in depicting lovely gardens. Just as the Garden of Eden was the finishing touch to the Creation, so have beautiful homes and estates of people throughout the ages needed beautiful gardens to provide the finishing touch. There is an air of peaceful repose in this 'Lovely Garden, Where Dreams Come True,' that suggests Romance and romantic dreams--and who isn't interested in romance? With the skill of the master that he is, R.A. Fox vividly portrays this colorful 'garden of dreams'--and what an ideal spot this presents for day dreaming and for building 'air castles.' R.A. Fox, son of Sarah Atkinson and Rev. Henry Fox, was born in Toronto, Canada. As a child, he was very delicate, but always showed a strong leaning toward Art. He was his own teacher until he entered the studio of J.W. Bridgeman, remaining with him about four years. Since that time, he has studied in London and Paris. He has exhibited exclusively in America. Although one of the more idealistic of American artists, he is proclaimed as having exceptional technique and the happy faculty of imparting a remarkable naturalness to his subjects. In presenting you with this calendar, we hope this garden scene will help to keep your home cheery and full of gladness and give you pleasure during the coming year." Courtesy Duane & Dolores Ramsey.

Fig. 155-a

(#635). Untitled. R.A. Fox. Below is printed, "Oh! Rare's the sunset when warm o'er the Lakes/Its splendor at the parting a miracle makes." 10 x 8. Courtesy Mary Battaglia.

(#558). "Dreamland." This exquisite scene shows a lovely brunette in a white gown standing near the bottom of a winding flower-bedecked staircase & staring dreamily out over the water at right. The viewer's distance from the autumn colors enhance the dreamlike quality. Elegant and refreshing. Sample calendar. 7 x 5. Courtesy Duane & Dolores Ramsey.

Fig. 156

Fig. 157

HOUSES, MILLS, FARM SCENES AND OTHER STRUCTURES

(#668). "Down Memory Lane." R.A. Fox. 7 x 9 1/2 calendar print. Courtesy Milan Royle.

Fig. 158

(#349). "Just a Place to Call Our Own." R.A. Fox. The American Art Works, Coshocton, Ohio. 7 x 9. Found on a 1931 calendar by Barbara Kern.

Fig. 159

(#380). Untitled. R.A. Fox. Brown tones dominate. 13 1/2 x 16 1/2, 20 x 26. Courtesy Pat Gibson.

Fig. 160

(#520). "It's Only A Cottage, But It's Home." Painting by R.A. Fox. ©. K.T.Co., Cin., Ohio. #31515. 9 x 12. Courtesy Duane & Dolores Ramsey. Also found as an advertising thermometer. #520 has also been found as a 7 1/2 x 9 calendar print, titled "Lakeside Cottage," and ©. O.H.K.

Fig. 161

#520 has also been found with the following printed on the back:

"It's Only a Cottage, But
It's Home"

From the original painting by R. Atkinson Fox
Copyright by THE KEMPER-THOMAS COMPANY
Cincinnati, Ohio

*"Mid pleasures and palaces
Tho we may roam,
Be it ever so humble
There's no place like home."*

Poets and writers say that the proper setting for "Home, Sweet Home" is a small cottage with thatched roof, surrounded by a colorful garden filled with beautiful flowers of every description, vines and stately trees.

Not grandeur, not ornate furnishings, not colonial pillars make a home—it's the association of memories that bless and burn, smiles and tears, the home-keeping hearts, the joys, the sorrows, the loves—all these come rushing back as we burn the incense of tender memories before the shrine of "Home."

R. Atkinson Fox, to whom we are indebted for this beautiful conception of "Home," has succeeded in conveying that "homey" atmosphere in his paintings, that constitutes the difference between just a house, and a "home."

Each detail in this painting is done with the skill of the master artist he is, and the coloring is an exact reproduction done so wonderfully by old Mother Nature, herself.

R. Atkinson Fox, son of Sarah Atkinson and Rev. Henry Fox, was born in Toronto, Canada. As a child he was very delicate, but always had a strong leaning toward Art. At the age of twelve, his health improved and he commenced the study of Art. He was his own teacher until he entered the studio of J. W. Bridgeman, remaining with him about four years. Since that time, he has studied in London and Paris. He has exhibited exclusively in America. Although one of the more idealistic of American artists, he is proclaimed as having exceptional technique and the happy faculty of imparting a remarkable naturalness to his subjects.

R. Atkinson Fox has won for himself an enviable reputation as a painter of pictures that re-create happy memories.

We hope this reproduction of the artist's conception of "Home" will prove interesting to you and give you as much pleasure during the coming year as we have in presenting it to you.

Fig. 161-a

Finally, #520 has been found as an 11 1/2 x 14 3/4. "Royal Puzzle" titled "Cottage Home." Courtesy Ben & Sandra Ross.

Fig. 161-b

(#636). "Rest Haven." Attributed to R.A. Fox in 1924 salesman's calendar portfolio of The Allen A. Co., Kenosha, Wisconsin. Listed size, 16 3/4 x 10 1/4. Other prints have been found in sizes, 8 x 10, 9 x 7, & 7 x 6. Courtesy John Jaegers.

Fig. 162

(#519). Untitled. (R.A. Fox.) The signature has only been found on a signed, original oil. A couple of unsigned prints have surfaced. In the lower left corner of one is printed, "By special permission of the copyright owners, Art Publishing Co., Chicago." In the lower right corner, "Printed in Prussia." Another has the same information except "Printed in Prussia" is stamped on the back. 12 x 16. This photo courtesy Ben & Sandra Ross. (Note: The scene in the oil extends farther on both sides.)

Fig. 163

(#603). "The Old Bridge." Unsigned (see pg. 142, Book I). 4 3/4 x 3 1/4. Courtesy Ben & Sandra Ross.

Fig. 164

(#399). "When the Day is Over." 1881. Painting by R.A. Fox. ©. F.A.S. (I think the "1881" here is a publisher's number, not a date.) 10 x 8. Courtesy Duane & Dolores Ramsey.

Fig. 165

(#657). "Crystal Falls." R.A. Fox. ©. 1920, The American Art Works, Coshocton, Ohio. This print is 2 3/4 x 3 1/2 on an overall 4 x 9 blotter. To the right of the print is a message: "If you return this blotter with your first order, we will allow Ten Dollars credit on the order. Commercial Lumber Co., Warren, Pa." Ten dollars was a lot of money in 1920, so probably a lot of these were sent in and subsequently destroyed. Courtesy Pat Gibson.

Fig. 166

(#412). "The Cottage by the Sea." R.A. Fox. 11 x 14 on a 1933 calendar. Courtesy Della Simmons.

Fig. 167

73

(#543). "A Silvery Pathway." R.A. Fox. 9 x 6. Courtesy Wm. C. & Becky Fox.

Fig. 168

(#504). "The Busy Mill." Same title as & very similar to #400. 6 x 11 1/2. Collection Ann Fox Mergenthaler. Photo by author.

Fig. 169

(#400). "The Busy Mill." R.A. Fox. Found on a 1914 calendar. 10 x 4. Courtesy Duane & Dolores Ramsey.

Fig. 170

(#563). "The Mill and the Birches." Painting by R.A. Fox. © F.A.S. 10 x 8. Courtesy Pat Gibson.

Fig. 171

74

(#693). "The Old Mill." R.A. Fox. The Lutz & Gould Co., Bur. Ia. 6 x 4 1/2. Courtesy Pat Gibson.

Fig. 172

(#411). "Homeward Bound." "©. Baumgarth, Chicago, painted by Fox." Print is captioned: "His corn & cattle were his only care, and his supreme delight a county fair." 5 1/2 x 3 1/2. Courtesy Barb Kratz.

Fig. 173

(#538). "The Old Mill." Painting by R.A. Fox. Found on a 1924 calendar by Mary Battaglia.

Fig. 174

(#394). "By the Old Mill Stream." #1741, ©. F.A.S. Painting by R.A. Fox. Also found on an advertising thermometer and a fan. 10 x 8. Courtesy Duane & Dolores Ramsey. Note: This has also been found attributed to "H. Whitroy."

Fig. 175

(#420). Untitled. I considered leaving this print out of the book, but I'd rather you were aware of it and the confusion surrounding it. I have seen a photograph of this print signed "R. Atkinson Fox" on the front. It has also been found on cardboard titled "Breath of Spring," by "Westal" and with "Winde Fine Prints" stamped on the back. This is also sometimes signed Westal on the front. Other examples have been found with stamped on the back: "Woodland Brook"

Robert Wood, Contemporary American

This is but one of the hundreds of landscapes painted by the famous Robert Wood during his career which spans more than 40 years.

Finally, it is advertised in the March, 1968, "Woman's Day" as "Stony Mill in Spring," one of "Four Magnificent Seasonal Landscapes" painted by "one of America's most popular landscape artists, Robert Westal." The prints were available from "The Homestead" on Madison Ave., N.Y. © RTV Sales Inc. The print shown is 9 1/2 x 14. Courtesy Barb Kratz.

Fig. 176

(#562). "The Curfew Tolls the Knell of Parting Day." R.A. Fox. This is a very dark print. At left is what looks like a Spanish church, complete with tower & rock wall. A man is walking on the road that runs past the house toward a small house. 5 x 7. Courtesy Barb Kratz.

Fig. 177

(#612). "Ruins of Ticonderoga." "Fox" printed underneath. Red Wing Pub. Co. Spanish ruins along a riverbank. Cows, sheep, flowers, & a winding path. 9 x 11. Courtesy Margene & Terry Petros.

Always At Your Service
STATE BANK OF HALSTAD
HALSTAD, MINNESOTA
1926   JANUARY   1926

Fig. 178

(#601). "The Old Meeting House". Unsigned (see pg. 142, Book I). 4 3/4 x 3 1/4. Courtesy Ben & Sandra Ross.

(#557). "Aces All." R.A. Fox. Print is 10 x 8. Found on a 1929 calendar. Courtesy Bill & Doris Richardson.

Fig. 179

Fig. 180

(#401). Untitled. R.A. Fox. 16 x 20. Courtesy Duane & Dolores Ramsey.

(#388). "After the Harvest." R.A. Fox. 8 x 10, 3 x 4, 3 1/2 x 5. Courtesy Deanna Hulse.

Fig. 181

Fig. 182

(#356). "After the Harvest." R.A. Fox. Publisher's #4536. © 1913, The T.D.M., Co., Red Oak, Ia. 7 x 9. Courtesy John & Darlene Boland. The following label appears on the back of one example: " 'After the Harvest.' Reproduced by color photography from an original oil painting by R.A. Fox. Educated in several American Schools of Art. Studio in Philadelphia, Pa. His work is highly esteemed both by connoisseurs of art and by the public in general. The present picture is a good example of the artist's work and shows his ability to depict farm scenes in an exceedingly naturalistic manner."

(#350). "Summertime at Grandpa's." R.A. Fox. From "GRIT," Williamsport, Pa. 8 x 11. Courtesy Lois Trimble.

Fig. 183

Fig. 184

MISCELLANEOUS PEOPLE

(#463). Untitled (This Print has been dubbed "Flight to Egypt" by collectors). R.A. Fox. 14 x 10. This is also reported on a 3-part folding hand fan and a one-part "stick" fan. Photo courtesy Duane & Dolores Ramsey.

(#395). "Discovery of the Mississippi, 1541." R.A. Fox. 11 x 14, 12 x 20. Courtesy Duane & Dolores Ramsey.

Fig. 185

Fig. 186

(#544). "Departure of Columbus." From painting by R.A. Fox. Sample Calendar. 8 1/2 x 12. Courtesy Mary Battaglia.

(#528). "Washington at Valley Forge." R.A. Fox. Hayes Litho Co., Buffalo, N.Y. 9 1/2 x 12 1/2. Courtesy Pat Gibson.

Fig. 187

Fig. 188

(#633). "Gage's Surrender." From Painting by R.A. Fox. 8 x 12. Courtesy Ruth & Dale Niemeier.

(#425). "First Raising of the Stars and Stripes at Valley Forge." 4066, Painting by R.A. Fox. Print is 8 x 10. Poster is 20 1/2 x 14. Courtesy Pat Gibson.

Fig. 189

Fig. 190

(#712). "Washington at Valley Forge." The People's Art Project list describes a monthly mailing series titled the "Washington Thrift Series" and mentions three prints done by Fox, one of which is this title. On the back of this print is found, "T.D.M. Co., Red Oak, Ia. Washington Thrift Series, PSM-CP-D-RC9576-8." 5 x 3 1/2. Courtesy Margene & Terry Petros.

(#328). "General 'Mad' Anthony at the Battle of Stoney Point." R.A. Fox. Promotional gift of the Francis W. Wack Insurance, Schwenksville, Pa. 9 x 12. Courtesy Stan Noreika.

Fig. 191

Fig. 192

(#443). "Shouting the Battle Cry of Freedom." From painting by R.A. Fox. 20554--The K.Y. Co., Cin., Ohio. Found on a 1920 calendar. 11 x 7 1/2, 22 x 16. Courtesy Pat Gibson.

Fig. 193

(#456). "There's a Light in the Window, It Shineth for Thee." R.A. Fox. Night scene. Young man in W.W.I uniform--rifle on back, suitcase in hand--walks toward house with lighted window. Courtesy Shirley Austin.

Fig. 194

(#327). "The Turn of the Tide--Americans at Chateau Thierry." R.A. Fox. This print was a promotional item from Francis W. Wack Insurance, Schweksville, Pa. 9 x 12. Courtesy Stan Noreika.

Fig. 195

(#644). "Taking a Trench." R.A. Fox. 16 x 20. Courtesy Pat Gibson.

Fig. 196

82

(#482). "The Right of Way." R.A. Fox. The owner of this print is convinced it is old and original. However, we know of one collector who had modern prints made from her oil and sold them. 6 x 8. Courtesy Barb Kratz.

Fig. 197

(#352). "The Pioneer." R.A. Fox. ©. 1913, Brown & Bigelow. Found on a 1914 Calendar by Sharon Gergen.

Fig. 198

(#345). "Good News." R.A. Fox. GH-5159, ©. 1911, Red Wing Adv. Co. 15 x 5. Courtesy Loretta Goad.

Fig. 199

(#355). "The Forest Ranger." R.A. Fox. 9 x 7 calendar print. Courtesy Sam Veazy.

Fig. 200

(#459). Untitled. R.A. Fox. 14 x 11. Courtesy Wm. C. & Becky Fox.

Fig. 201

(#466). "Through the Mountain Pass." R.A. Fox. Also, "Painted by R. Atkinson Fox." ©. 1916, C.T.W., No. 102. (See L.C. listing, pg. 141 Book I.) 10 x 8. Also, 1917 Calendar. Courtesy Mary Battaglia.

Fig. 202

(#465). "First Tourists Visit Old Faithful." R.A. Fox, Northern Pacific Artist. This scene of a stagecoach stopped while its passengers gaze at the geyser may be the end result of the sketch on pg. 24 in Book I. 15 x 9. Courtesy Duane & Dolores Ramsey.

Fig. 203

(#710). "The Iron Horse--Driving the Golden Spike." T.D. Murphy Co., Red Oak, Ia. (Identified as RAF on People's Art Project list, from 1929.) This example is titled and unsigned. 18 1/2 x 24 1/2. Courtesy Margene & Terry Petros.

Fig. 204

(#702). "The Journey's End--Oregon." (Identified as RAF from "People's Art Project" list.) Thos. D. Murphy Co., Red Oak, Ia. 15 7/8 x 21 3/4. Courtesy Ben & Sandra Ross.

Fig. 205

(#642). "Their Attack Conquered." From Painting by R.A. Fox. 6 x 8, 9 x 12. Courtesy Pat Gibson.

Fig. 207

(#719). "By the Campfire Glow." Attributed to RAF in Red Wing Paintings Book. We may have discovered another pseudonym here. The Painting is signed "Leroy" & under the print is written " 12 x 36. By the Campfire Glow. Oil, Fox (Leroy)." The print is 15 x 5. The original oil was 36 x 12; no price is given. Courtesy Margene & Terry Petros.

Fig. 206

(#634). Untitled. R. Atkinson Fox. ©. 1916. Wonderfully unique & complex, this print apparently advertises "Es-ki-mo Brand Rubbers" made by McElwain Barton Shoe Co., Kansas City, Mo. U.S.A. (Written on wooden box.) 7 x 10 1/2. Courtesy Paul Stillwell.

Fig. 208

(#347). Untitled. R.A. Fox. 6 x 8. In memory of Norm Berube.

Fig. 209

(#548). Untitled. R.A. Fox. 22 x 17 1/2 framed puzzle. Also found as a print. Courtesy Pat Gibson.

Fig. 210

(#641). "Come Along My Beauty." R.A. Fox. Thos. D. Murphy Co., G-81396, Oct. 5, 1927. (Publishers info. comes from LC listing, pg. 141, Book I.) Sample calendar. 6 x 8. Courtesy Ben & Sandra Ross.

Fig. 211

(#571). "Smooth Sailing." R. Atkinson Fox. 8 x 6. Salesman's sample calendar. Courtesy Ben & Sandra Ross.

Fig. 212

(#708). "Oh Susanna--The Covered Wagon." Identified as RAF on the People's Art Project list, from 1928. This example is titled but not signed. 5 1/2 x 8. Courtesy Margene & Terry Petros.

Fig. 213

(#599). Untitled. R.A. Fox. © 1907, R. Hill. This is a dark print. 16 x 20. Courtesy Barb Kratz.

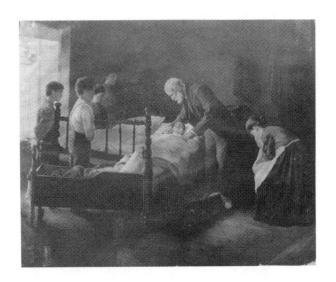

Fig. 214

(#701). "Down on Grandpa's Farm." From painting by R.A. Fox. Publisher's Number, 22322. The K.T. Co., Cin'ti, Ohio. 11 x 7 1/2. Courtesy Margene & Terry Petros.

Fig. 215

(#444). Untitled. R.A. Fox. Great car in backround! 7 x 9. Also, 7 x 9 signed, wooden puzzle. Courtesy Pat Gibson.

(#602). "The Old Well." Unsigned (see pg. 143, Book I). 4 3/4 x 3 1/4. Courtesy Ben & Sandra Ross.

Fig. 216

Fig. 217

(#533). "Faithful and True." R.A. Fox. 7 1/2 x 5 1/2. Courtesy Pat Gibson.

(#534). "The Best Piemaker in Town." R.A. Fox. © by R. Hill, 1905. 5 1/2 x 7 1/2. Courtesy Pat Gibson.

Fig. 218

Fig. 219

(#398). "My Boy." R.A. Fox. 7 x 9. Courtesy Duane & Dolores Ramsey.

(#671). "Between Two Fires." R.A. Fox. "From Painting by Fox." ©. 1909, Gerlach-Barklow. 7 x 10. Courtesy Pat Gibson.

Fig. 220

Fig. 221

(#503). Untitled. R. Atkinson Fox. 7 x 9. Courtesy Duane & Dolores Ramsey.

(#392). "Where Brooks Send Up a Cheerful Tune." #2263. R.A. Fox. 20 x 16, 14 x 11, 8 x 16. WARNING: This print is reproduced--in 16 x 20 & "guaranteed to look old." Courtesy Pat Gibson.

Fig. 222

Fig. 223

(#545). "Gosh!" (R) A. Fox. The signature at lower left is "A. Fox," but it is the signature of RAF with the "R" cut off--it is not the sterile, printed "A. Fox" we usually associate with the Hoover entity. 8 x 6. Courtesy Pat Gibson.

(#714). "Spirit of Discovery." Identified as RAF on People's Art Project list, from 1931. Under the cameo is, "Air Mail Saves Time/R.E. Byrd." This example is unsigned. 7 1/2 x 10. Courtesy Margene & Terry Petros.

Fig. 224

Fig. 225

(#734). "The Lone Eagle." (Title is under mat) Verified RAF by the People's Art Project [P.A.P.], Red Oak, Ia. Printed under the inset of Lindbergh is "Use the Air Mail/Charles A. Lindbergh". 6 x 8. Courtesy Pat Gibson.

(#736). "Out of the Sky He Comes." Identified as RAF in the People's Art Project (PAP) list. Illustrated here is a vividly-colored print from a 1932, Thos. D. Murphy Co. sample calendar.
10 1/2 x 7 1/2. Courtesy Margene & Terry Petros.

Fig. 226

Fig. 227

(#686). "Portrait of George Washington." Painting by R.A. Fox. ©. 1930, The American Art Works, Inc., Coshocton, Ohio. Found on a 1932 adv. calendar, 48 7/8 x 25--image is 22 5/8 x 18. Also found on a fan. Courtesy Ben & Sandra Ross.

The same portrait of George Washington was published on the January edition of T. D. Murphy Co.'s "Secrets of Success' Monthly Service Series" in 1923. 8 x 5. Courtesy People's Art Project, and JII/Sales Promotion Associates, Red Oak, Iowa.

Fig. 228

Fig. 228-a

(#740). "Abraham Lincoln." This portrait appeared on the February edition of Thos. D. Murphy Co.'s "Secrets of Success' Monthly Service Series" in 1923. 8 x 5. Courtesy People's Art Project, and JII/Sales Promotion Associates, Red Oak, Iowa.

(#741). "Theodore Roosevelt." This portrait appeared on the March edition of Thos. D. Murphy Co.'s "Secrets of Success' Monthly Service Series" in 1923. 8 x 5. Courtesy People's Art Project, and JII/Sales Promotion Associates, Red Oak, Iowa.

Fig. 229

Fig. 230

(#742). "Andrew Jackson." This portrait appeared on the April edition of Thos. D. Murphy Co.'s "Secrets of Success' Monthly Service Series" in 1923. 8 x 5. Courtesy People's Art Project, and JII/Sales Promotion Associates, Red Oak, Iowa.

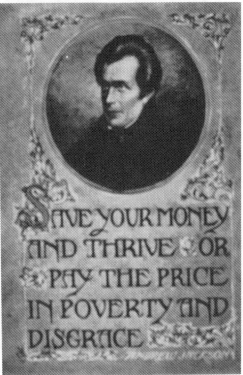

Fig. 231

(#743). "Andrew Carnegie." This portrait appeared on the May edition of Thos. D. Murphy Co.'s "Secrets of Success' Monthly Service Series" in 1923. 8 x 5. Courtesy People's Art Project, and JII/Sales Promotion Associates, Red Oak, Iowa.

Fig. 232

The portrait of Andrew Carnegie (Fig. 232) also appears on a blotter with the financial statement of the "Bank of Boyceville." It carries the same maxim as the calendar, and it was also published by the Thos. D. Murphy Co., Red Oak, Iowa. Courtesy Pat Gibson.

Fig. 232-a

(#744). "Benjamin Franklin." This portrait appeared on the June edition of Thos. D. Murphy Co.'s "Secrets of Success' Monthly Service Series" in 1923. 8 x 5. Courtesy People's Art Project, and JII/Sales Promotion Associates, Red Oak, Iowa.

Fig. 233

(#745). "Marshall Field." This portrait appeared on the July edition of Thos. D. Murphy Co.'s "Secrets of Success' Monthly Service Series" in 1923. 8 x 5. Courtesy People's Art Project, and JII/Sales Promotion Associates, Red Oak, Iowa.

Fig. 234

(#746). "James J. Hill." This portrait appeared on the August edition of Thos. D. Murphy Co.'s "Secrets of Success' Monthly Service Series" in 1923. 8 x 5. Courtesy People's Art Project, and JII/Sales Promotion Associates, Red Oak, Iowa.

Fig. 235

(#711). "Grover Cleveland." This portrait appeared on the September edition of Thos. D. Murphy Co.'s "Secrets of Success Monthly Mailing Series" in 1923. It is not signed or titled. The print is 5 x 3 1/2 & the entire calendar is 10 x 5 1/2. Courtesy Pat Gibson.

Fig. 236

(#747). "Sir Thomas Lipton." This portrait appeared on the October edition of Thos. D. Murphy Co.'s "Secrets of Success' Monthly Service Series" in 1923. 8 x 5. Courtesy People's Art Project, and JII/Sales Promotion Associates, Red Oak, Iowa.

Fig. 237

(#748). "Philip D. Armour." This portrait appeared on the November edition of Thos. D. Murphy Co.'s "Secrets of Success' Monthly Service Series" in 1923. 8 x 5. Courtesy People's Art Project, and JII/Sales Promotion Associates, Red Oak, Iowa.

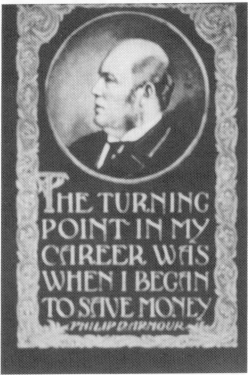

Fig. 238

(#749). "Warren Harding." This portrait appeared on the November edition of Thos. D. Murphy Co.'s "Secret of Success' Monthly Service Series" in 1923. 8 x 5. Courtesy People's Art Project, and JII/Sales Promotion Associates, Red Oak, Iowa.

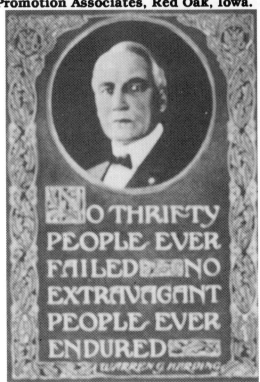

Fig. 239

(#700). "Abraham Lincoln." (Identified as RAF on "People's Art Project" list. According to the P.A.P.") T.D. Murphy Co. A Calendar for Winona Store Co./General Merchants/Winona, Ohio. Image is 10 7/8 x 8 3/8. Courtesy Ben & Sandra Ross.

Fig. 240

(#750). "Gutenberg." The printing press and its inventor appeared on the January issue of Thos. D. Murphy's 'Great Inventions' Monthly Service Series" for 1924. Courtesy People's Art Project, and JII/Sales Promotion Associates, Red Oak, Iowa.

Fig. 241

(#751). "George Stevenson." The locomotive and its inventor appeared on the February issue of Thos. D. Murphy's "'Great Inventions' Monthly Service Series" for 1924. Courtesy People's Art Project, and JII/Sales Promotion Associates, Red Oak, Iowa.

Fig. 242

(#752). "Elias Howe." The sewing machine and its inventor were featured on the March issue of Thos. D. Murphy's "'Great Inventions' Monthly Service Series" for 1924. Courtesy People's Art Project, and JII/Sales Promotion Associates, Red Oak, Iowa.

Fig. 243

(#753). "James Watt." The man who refined the steam engine for practical use appeared on the April issue of Thos. D. Murphy's "'Great Inventions' Monthly Service Series" for 1924. Courtesy People's Art Project, and JII/Sales Promotion Associates, Red Oak, Iowa.

Fig. 244

(#754). "Eli Whitney." The inventor of the cotton gin appeared on the May issue of Thos. D. Murphy's "'Great Inventions' Monthly Service Series" for 1924. Courtesy People's Art Project, and JII/Sales Promotion Associates, Red Oak, Iowa.

Fig. 245

(#755). "Cyrus McCormick." The reaper and its inventor were featured on the June issue of Thos. D. Murphy's "'Great Inventions' Monthly Service Series" for 1924. Courtesy People's Art Project, and JII/Sales Promotion Associates, Red Oak, Iowa.

Fig. 246

(#756). "Robert Fulton." The man who brought the steam boat into practical use is honored on the July issue of Thos. D. Murphy's "'Great Inventions' Monthly Service Series" for 1924. Courtesy People's Art Project, and JII/Sales Promotion Associates, Red Oak, Iowa.

Fig. 247

(#757). "Samuel Morse." The inventor of the telegraph is featured on the August issue of Thos. D. Murphy's "'Great Inventions' Monthly Service Series" for 1924. Courtesy People's Art Project, and JII/Sales Promotion Associates, Red Oak, Iowa.

Fig. 248

(#758). "Alexander Bell." The man responsible for those telephone bills we get every month looks shamelessly out from the September issue of Thos. D. Murphy's "'Great Inventions' Monthly Service Series" for 1924. Courtesy People's Art Project, and JII/Sales Promotion Associates, Red Oak, Iowa.

Fig. 249

(#759). "Thomas Edison." The great inventor shows up on the October issue of Thos. D. Murphy's "'Great Inventions' Monthly Service Series" for 1924. Courtesy People's Art Project, and JII/Sales Promotion Associates, Red Oak, Iowa.

Fig. 250

(#760). "Marconi." The inventor behind wireless communication is honored on the November issue of Thos. D. Murphy's "'Great Inventions' Monthly Service Series" for 1924. Courtesy People's Art Project, and JII/Sales Promotion Associates, Red Oak, Iowa.

(#761). "Wilbur Wright." One of the famous flying brothers is shown with a wonderful old biplane on the December issue of Thos. D. Murphy's "'Great Inventions' Monthly Service Series" for 1924. Courtesy People's Art Project, and JII/Sales Promotion Associates, Red Oak, Iowa.

Fig. 252

Fig. 251

NATIVE AMERICANS

(#376). "Flower of the Forest." Signed. The Osborne Co. It's hard to believe, but in all this time since Book I, we've only listed one Indian maiden. 1925 calendar. 16 x 10, 8 x 6 1/2. Courtesy Donna Robinson.

(#450). Untitled. R.A. Fox. Courtesy Pat Gibson.

Fig. 253

Fig. 254

(#565). "The Sky Line." R.A. Fox. Indians on horseback are barely visible on a distant cliff in the far right background. 9 x 7. Ramsey.

(#687). Untitled. R.A. Fox. You probably won't be able to see him in the illustration, but there's an Indian on horseback at the base of the two bluffs. 10 1/4 x 8 1/2. Courtesy Della Simmons.

Fig. 255

Fig. 256

99

(#354). Untitled. R.A. Fox. An Indian is rowing a canoe at lower left, and a bear is visible at right-- below the deer. 9 x 12. Courtesy Hugh Hetzer.

(#632). "Good Guide." Painting by R.A. Fox. This looks like a detail from the next print. However, there are slight differences between this Indian and the central figure in #670. Courtesy Duane & Dolores Ramsey.

Fig. 257

Fig. 258

(#670). Untitled. R.A. Fox. 4 1/2 x 12. Courtesy Ben & Sandra Ross.

Fig. 259

Here is a close-up of the central figure in #670, for comparison to "Good Guide."
Courtesy Ben & Sandra Ross.

Fig. 259-a

(#389). "Old Faithful by Moonlight." R.A. Fox. Northern Pacific artist. (Attribution at bottom right.) 15 x 9. Collection Ann Fox Mergenthaler. Photo by author.

"Old Faithful by Moonlight" has also been found on a 1951-52 calendar by The Thos. D. Murphy Co. Courtesy Nick Morin.

Fig. 260

Fig. 260-a

(#631). "In the Foothills." R. A .Fox. ©. 1910 by Chas Williams, N.Y. 6 1/2 x 10.
Ann Fox Mergenthaler collection. Photo by author.

Fig. 261

(#703). "H119-In the Days of '49." Atkinson. (Number, title, and name are printed in margin under picture.) 1926, Red Wing calendar sample. A wagon train is visible, stretched out under a crescent moon on a hilltop in the background. (Margene points out that this is on a Red Wing sample identical to the one in #612 which is identified as "H119-Fox." This one is identified as H119-Atkinson.)
Courtesy Margene & Terry Petros.

Fig. 262

CHILDREN

(#339). Untitled. R.A. Fox. (Could that crooked picture with the familiar blue be an early Fox?) 9 1/2 x 7 1/2. Courtesy Loretta Goad.

Fig. 263

(#722). "You Shan't Go Swimming, So There!" Marked "2497 Fox." Also attributed to RAF in the People's Art Project (P.A.P.) files. This example is on a 1909 calendar advertising "Sabins Educational Exchange," a "Teacher's Agency" in Des Moines. (Also see Painting Record #51/471, pg.42, Book I.) Print is 2 3/4 x 2. Calendar is 6 1/4 x 3 1/2. Courtesy Pat Gibson.

Fig. 264

(#640). "Repairing of All Kinds." R.A. Fox. H-306. © C.E. South. 13 x 10. Courtesy Pat Gibson.

Fig. 265

(#396). "Ring Around Rosy." R.A. Fox. 5 x 7. Courtesy Duane & Dolores Ramsey.

Fig. 266

(#585). "Please Don't Make Us Go to Bed." R.A. Fox. ©. The Osborne Co., Newark, N.J., and Toronto, Ont. (1921--see L.C. list, pg. 143, Book I.) 8 x 7. Courtesy Pat Gibson.

Fig. 267

(#322). "A Safe Companion." R.A. Fox. ©. 1910, R. Hill. You might not be able to see the lady in a long white dress in the far left background. 7 x 10. Courtesy Barbara Kern.

Fig. 268

(#623). Untitled. Painting by R.A. Fox. Notice the ship on the horizon. Found on a 1921 calendar. 14 x 11. Courtesy Pat Gibson.

Fig. 269

(#639). "Satisfaction Guaranteed." Painting by R. Atkinson Fox. ©. B.F. Haskin, Chicago. Courtesy Barb Kratz.

Fig. 270

(#501). Untitled. R.A. Fox. 9 x 6. Courtesy Duane Dolores Ramsey.

(#621). "Faith." R.A. Fox. 11 x 8 1/2. Courtesy Pat Gibson.

Fig. 271

Fig. 272

(#684). "Among the Daisies--6727." From Painting by Fox. © 1904, TDM Co. Also found in a 1907 Thos. D. Murphy Co. catalog. See Painting Record #37, pg. 43, Book I. 7 1/4 x 10 1/4. Courtesy Margene & Terry Petros.

(#378). Untitled. R.A. Fox. Young girl in white suit & hat, playing golf. 9 x 3. Courtesy Wm. C. & Becky Fox.

Fig. 273

Fig. 274

(#379). Untitled. R.A. Fox. 9 x 3. Courtesy Wm. C. & Becky Fox.

Fig. 275

(#683). "6712--ONE STRIKE--FOX." ©. 1905, TDM Co. Photographed from a 1907 Thos. D. Murphy Co. catalog. See Painting Record #207, pg. 42, Book I. Kratz.

Fig. 276

(#638). "A Life Saver." R. Atkinson Fox. Courtesy Barb Kratz.

Fig. 277

(#681). "4941 Me and Rex." From painting by Fox. ©. 1907, Thos. D. Murphy Co., Red Oak, Iowa. This print was photographed from a TDM Co. catalog. The catalog caption reads, "Me and Rex". Reproduced from an original painting by the same artist as "The Fish Story." Courtesy Barb Kratz.

Fig. 278

(#637). "Warm Friends." Publishers #29576. "Reproduced from original canvas by R.A. Fox. © Louis F. Dow Co." 16 x 11. This has also been found on a titled, 14 x 10, "Big Star" puzzle, and as half of a "Perfect Double" puzzle. Courtesy Ben & Sandra Ross.

(#342). "The Barefoot Boy." Also, "Pals." Signed. Notice that this boy's face, hair, pose--everything except his hat and clothes color is identical to the child in "Warm Friends." Found on a Scrapbook cover and as advertising for "Cottage Loaf" at Corkshank's Bakery, Chillicothe, Mo. 16 x 11. Also found on an unsigned, 15 x 10. 275-piece puzzle. Courtesy Pat Gibson.

Fig. 279

Fig. 280

(#622). "Prepared." Painting by R.A. Fox. © F.A.S. 4018. 8 1/4 x 11 1/4. Courtesy Pat Gibson.

(#384). "Down by the Bridge." R. Atkinson Fox. 7 1/2 x 6 1/2. Also found on adv. thermometer, and in 7 x 9 1/2 on a 1932 adv. calendar. Courtesy Deanna Hulse.

Fig. 281

Fig. 282

(#682). "4942--The Fish Story." From painting by Fox. ©. 1907, Thos. D. Murphy Co., Red Oak, Ia. This is from the same TDM Co. catalog as #681, "Me & Rex." The catalog caption reads: "The Fish Story. A new tale for a twentieth-century edition of the Arabian Nights, caught at the moment of first narration by the skillful brush of Mr. Fox. 'Chimmy' has just returned from an excursion to the country, and is unfolding to a trio of eager friends the wonderful story of a mighty fish he has caught unaided. R. Atkinson Fox is a clever American artist, whose power lies in his ability to depict facial expressions and in his carefulness to detail. During the last few years he has retired from active work, and pictures from his brush are now exeedingly hard to obtain. This same subject is shown as a large roll calendar on page 51." Picture from a 1909 calendar. Courtesy Barb Kratz.

Fig. 283

(#597). "Look Pretty." From painting by R.A. Fox. ©. E.N. H-2432. 11 x 8. Courtesy Pat Gibson.

(#721). "Mother's Joy." Attributed to RAF in Red Wing Paintings Book. Red-headed mother in yellow dress lifts baby in blue romper. Oil is described as 30 x 24. Price is cut off. Print is 5 x 3, 8 x 6. Courtesy Margene & Terry Petros.

Fig. 284

Fig. 285

109

(#709). "An Armful of Joy." R.A. Fox. © John Baumgarth Co., Chicago. 10 x 8. Courtesy Wm. C. & Becky Fox.

Fig. 286

(#720). "Mutual Affections." R. Atkinson Fox. Courtesy Ron & Frieda Clark.

Fig. 287

(#664). "American Madonna." From Oil Painting by R.A. Fox. © 1906, Sparrell Art Co. Engraved & Printed by The Sparrell Print, Boston. 21 x 17. Courtesy Wm. C. & Becky Fox.

Fig. 288

(#630). "Baby's First Tooth." From Painting by R.A. Fox. © E.N. H-2467. 14 x 9 1/2. Courtesy Pat Gibson.

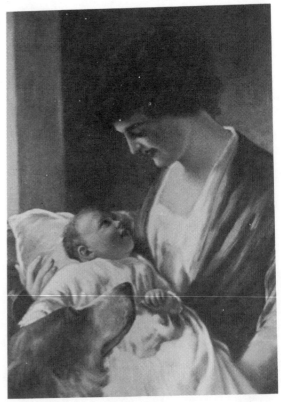

Fig. 289

110

BEAUTIFUL YOUNG WOMEN

(#436). "Dream Castle." Publisher's number 823. Painting by R.A. Fox. ©. F.A.S. Found on a 1931 calendar--print 12 x 10. Also found on an undated "hard" calendar--10 x 8. Courtesy Pat Gibson.

Fig. 290

(#410). "Day Dreams." R. Atkinson Fox. ©. Louis F. Dow Co. 11 x 14. 5 x 7. Courtesy Barb Kratz.

Fig. 291

Here is "Day Dreams" on a 10 1/4 x 13 1/2 "Big Star" puzzle titled "Harbor Villa." The signature is only partially visible at the bottom right. Courtesy Wm. C. & Becky Fox.

Fig. 291-a

"Day Dreams" has also been found as 1/2 of "Perfect Double Puzzle" with "River of Romance" (Fig. 160, Book I) as the "mystery" bottom picture. Puzzle picture from author's collection.

Fig. 291-b

(#738). "My Castle of Dreams." Painting by R.A. Fox. K.T. Co., 1930, #30885. Compare this young lady's pose to that of #70 (Fig. 227, Book I). That's a rose she is holding, and a castle is visible at upper left. This is also found as an advertising thermometer. 9 x 14. Courtesy Margene & Terry Petros.

Fig. 292

(#575). "Oriental Dreams." By R. Atkinson Fox. This print has been found titled on the front and with the following information on the back:
"Oriental Dreams"
by R. Atkinson Fox.
R. Atkinson Fox is an American painter who now resides in the city of Chicago. He has had a long and successful career in painting landscapes, marine and figure subjects. His works are well known to practically every American publisher as he has been very fortunate in having his paintings reproduced. The scene, "Oriental Dreams," is taken from an actual villa in the Orient, placed in a fortified position high on the cliffs. The villa has a beautiful and commanding view. Mr. Fox has artistically inserted a dancing girl, which adds life and interest to his painting. 9 x 12. Courtesy Pat Gibson.

Fig. 293

(#598). "The Gates of Dreamland." Unsigned. A gorgeous print of the painting shown in Fig. 30, Book I. Sunlit trees & fantasy city in background-- Viking ship rowing on blue, blue water. 14 x 10 1/2. Courtesy Duane & Dolores Ramsey.

Fig. 294

(#716). "Meditation." Attributed to RAF in Red Wing Paintings Book. Oil is listed as 30 x 24 and $150. Print is 8 1/2 x 6 1/2. Courtesy Margene & Terry Petros.

Fig. 295

(#717). "Water Lilies." Attributed to RAF in Red Wing Paintings Book. Oil is 24 x 30 & was listed at $150. Print is 3 x 5. Courtesy Margene & Terry Petros.

Fig. 296

(#500). "The Valley of Enchantment." Painting by R.A. Fox. ©. The K.T. Co., Cin'ti, Ohio. 13 x 10. An unusual example has been found with this print on both sides of a 10 1/2 x 8 1/2 print. Both sides are titled, but only one side carries "Painting by R.A. Fox." Courtesy Duane & Dolores Ramsey.

Fig. 297

(#706). "Spirit of the Harvest." This will be a favorite--hope more are out there. 8 x 6. Courtesy Margene & Terry Petros.

(#364). "A Fair Skipper." R.A. Fox. H.L. Young Co. Found on a 1918 calendar. 9 x 4 1/2. Courtesy Ron & Bernie Shaw.

Fig. 298

Fig. 299

(#669). "Oriental Beauties." R.A. Fox. ©. 1903, Fred C. Lounsbury. RAF must have done a series of this type of work. This is so similar to #629, and I have several of this type of work. This is so similar to #629, and I have several others of the same genre in "Unsigned Maybes." This was found on a 1906 calendar in sizes 5 x 7 and 8 x 10. Courtesy Pat Gibson.

(#629). Untitled. R.A. Fox. © 1902, C.K. Groves, Phila. 7 x 9. Courtesy Pat Gibson.

Fig. 300

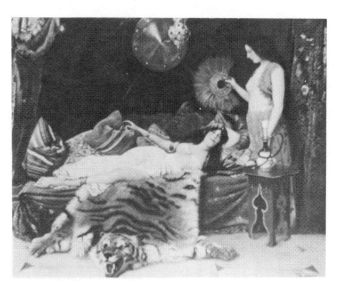

Fig. 301

(#595). "The Village Belle." R. Atkinson Fox. ©. 1900 by J. Hoover & Sons, Phila. 22 x 28. Courtesy Ron & Clare Santelli.

Fig. 302

(#718). "Mid Flowers Fair." Attributed to RAF in Red Wing Paintings Book. Oil was listed at $150. Print is 5 x 3, 6 x 8. Courtesy Margene & Terry Petros.

Fig. 303

(#517). "Ruth." R. Atkinson Fox. © 1905 by Fred C. Lounsbury. 11 x 8 1/2. Courtesy Duane & Dolores Ramsey.

Fig. 304

(#596). "Maud Muller." By R.A. Fox. John Palmer Co., Philadelphia. Found on a postcard--print size is 3 1/2 x 2 1/2. ("Maud Muller" is the title and subject of one of the best-known poems by Henry Greenleaf Whittier. "Maud Muller on a summer's day\Raked the meadow sweet with hay...") Courtesy Pat Gibson.

Fig. 305

(#685). "Sweet Memories." Painting by R.A. Fox. ©. F.A.S. Beautiful profile portrait of a young brunette in a white hat & red garment with white collar. Found on a 20 x 15 salesman's sample calendar-- image size, 10 1/2 x 10 5/8. Courtesy Ben & Sandra Ross

(#467). "Meditation." R. Atkinson Fox. 11 x 8. Courtesy Duane & Dolores Ramsey.

Fig. 306

Fig. 307

(#468). "Roses Fair." R.A. Fox. This beautiful brunette clutches a bouquet of pink roses. 13 x 10. Courtesy Duane & Dolores Ramsey.

(#715). "Glory of Youth." Attributed to RAF in Red Wing Paintings Book. Oil was listed at 23 3/4 x 17 3/4 & $150. print is 8 x 6, 16 x 20. Courtesy Margene & Terry Petros.

Fig. 308

Fig. 309

117

BEAUTIFUL YOUNG WOMEN WITH HORSES, ONE COW, AND A DOG

(#666). "Attractions of the Farm." R. Atkinson Fox. 11 x 8. Courtesy Ben & Sandra Ross.

(#665). Untitled. R. Atkinson Fox. 15 x 9. Courtesy Pat Gibson.

Fig. 310

Fig. 311

(#656). "Faithful and True." Painting by R. Atkinson Fox. Courtesy John Jaegers.

(#643). "A Thrilling Moment." R. Atkinson Fox. 6 1/2 x 8 1/4. Collection Ann Fox Megenthaler. Photo by author.

Fig. 312

Fig. 313

(#628). "Companions." R.A. Fox. Cover of 1918 Seneca County Press Almanac, Pub. by Seneca Press Co., Seneca Falls, N.Y. Print is 5 1/4 x 3 3/4. Courtesy Hugh Hetzer.

Fig. 314

(#582). "Friends." From painting by R.A. Fox. ©. E.N. H-3055. 11 1/2 x 8 1/2. Courtesy Pat Gibson.

Fig. 315

(#574). "The Girl of the Golden West." ©. 1911 by R.A. Fox. The Osborne Co., N.Y. 9 x 6. Courtesy Pat Gibson.

Fig. 316

(#573). "Ready for a Cantor." R.A. Fox. ©. 1909 by Chas. Williams. 11 x 8. Courtesy Pat Gibson.

Fig. 317

"Ready for a Cantor" has also been found on a postcard with a distinctive format. Two other postcards with this same format are (center) Fig. 255, Book I, and (right) an "Unsigned Maybe,"

Fig. 317-a

(#581). "Fooling Him." R.A. Fox. ©. 1909 by Chas. Williams, N.Y. This lovely lady is offering the horse an apple and concealing a halter behind her back. 6 x 8. Courtesy Pat Gibson.

(#546). Untitled. R.A. Fox. This beautiful young redhead reminds me of "Fergie," the current Princess of York. 9 1/4 x 7. Courtesy Wm C. & Becky Fox.

Fig. 318

Fig. 319

(#547). "The Reward." R. Atkinson Fox. ©. F.A. Schneider. 1917 sample calendar. 9 3/4 x 7 3/4. Courtesy Duane & Dolores Ramsey.

Fig. 320

(#383). "A Treat." R. Atkinson Fox. ©. F.A. Schneider. 9 x 11 1/2. Courtesy Deanna Hulse.

Fig. 321

(#513). "The Treat." R. Atkinson Fox. Salesman's sample calendar. 7 x 5. Courtesy Pat Gibson.

Fig. 322

(#512). "Thoroughbreds." R. Atkinson Fox. Cover of the 1912 "Mifflenburg Telegraph Almanac." 5 x 4. Courtesy Pat Gibson.

Fig. 323

Fig. 468

Fig. 193

Fig. 261

Fig. 412

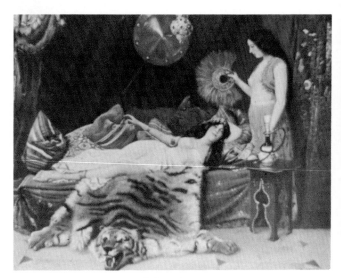

Fig. 301

Fig. 281

Fig. 439

Fig. 150

Fig. 446

Fig. 336

Fig. 226

Fig. 365

Fig. 196

Fig. 3

Fig. 56

Fig. 17

Fig. 27

Fig. 62

Fig. 41

Fig. 45

Fig. 42

Fig. 47

Fig. 57

Fig. 58

Fig. 53

Fig. 36

Fig. 59

Fig. 61

Fig. 52

Fig. 54

Fig. 24

Fig. 49

Fig. 15

Fig. 32

Fig. 35

Fig. 22

Fig. 37

Fig. 43-a

Fig. 55

Fig. 23

Fig. 46

Fig. 44

Fig. 29

Fig. 14

Fig. 51

Fig. 48

Fig. 21

Fig. 40

Fig. 18

Fig. 38

Fig. 26

Fig. 25

Fig. 39

Fig. 50

Fig. 331

Fig. 405

Fig. 313

Fig. 213

Fig. 208

Fig. 263

Fig. 333

"Thoroughbreds" has also been found on the cover of the "1921 St. Cloud Daily Times Almanac." Below the picture is printed, "Times Publishing Co., St. Cloud, Minn." Print size is 5 1/4 x 3 3/4. Courtesy Barb Kratz.

Fig. 323-a

(#470). Untitled. R.A. Fox. ©. 1907 by Fred C. Lounsbury. Courtesy Duane & Dolores Ramsey.

Fig. 324

(#723). Untitled. R.A. Fox. Publisher--Chas. Williams. This cart has wonderful red wheels. 7 x 10. Courtesy Margene & Terry Petros.

Fig. 325

(#499). Untitled. R. Atkinson Fox. 12 x 8. Courtesy Duane & Dolores Ramsey.

Fig. 326

123

(#397). "Faithful Friends." R. Atkinson Fox. 10 x 8. Courtesy Duane & Dolores Ramsey.

Fig. 327

(#375). "Her Pet." R.A. Fox. Found on a 1917 adv. calendar. 11 1/2 x 8 1/2, 8 x 6. Courtesy Wm. C. & Becky Fox.

Fig. 328

(#367). Untitled. R.A. Fox. © 1904 by H. Kenyon. 8 x 6. Courtesy Ron & Bernie Shaw.

Fig. 329

(#341). "Deering." R.A. Fox. © International Harvester Co. The trademark "IHC" can be seen on the gate. "Deering" at top. Adv. print. 20 1/2 x 13 1/2. Courtesy Nowotny collection.

Fig. 330

(#338). Untitled. R. Atkinson Fox. 12 x 8. Courtesy Loretta Goad.

(#724). "Three Friends." Attributed to RAF in Red Wing Paintings Book. Oil is 29 1/2 x 23 1/2 & was listed at $100. Print is 11 x 8. Courtesy Margene & Terry Petros.

Fig. 331

Fig. 332

Fig. 333

Fig. 334

HORSES

(#627). "Good Luck." R. Atkinson Fox. ©. 1902 by Fred C. Lounsbury. The signature is on the left tip of the horseshoe. 7 x 5. Courtesy Margene & Terry Petros.

Fig. 335

(#688). "Duke." R.A. Fox. 1918, Brown & Bigelow, U.S.A. S. Sault Ste. Marie Ont. 19536 from Painting by R. Atkinson Fox. Found on a 1920 calendar. Print is 12 x 11. Courtesy Pat Gibson.

Fig. 336

(#428). "Ready for All Comers." (Print has been trimmed or was not printed in its entirety--only visible part of the signature is "Fox." But it's RAF's signature.) Looks like a racetrack in the far background. 14 x 11, 19 x 14. Courtesy JoAnn Mangskau.

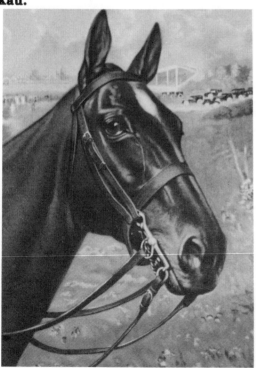

Fig. 337

(#739). "The Horse Pasture." On page 43, Book I, Painting Record #71 shows a painting titled "The Horse Pasture." The artist is listed as R.A. Fox, Philadelphia, with "After Chialiva" written above. As series number 4315, it is shown to have been reproduced by the Electrotint Engraving Co. This painting is illustrated in a 1904 catalog of the Thos. D. Murphy Co. with the following caption: "The Horse Pasture" is a copy painted for the Thos D. Murphy Co. of a famous painting by the Italian Chialiva. A print has been found with the Italian name spelled "Chiliva." 4 1/2 x 8 1/2. From a catalog owned by Margene & Terry Petros. Photo by author.

Fig. 338

(#583). "Tom & Jerry." Sgnd. R.A. Fox, and "From painting by R.A. Fox" is printed in the margin. (By the way, this title does not refer to the cartoon cat and mouse any more than the T & J punch sets do. Tom & Jerry were a well-known pair of vaudeville-type comedians. Most of those punch sets and certainly this print predate the cartoon which was created in 1939.) 9 x 12. Courtesy Pat Gibson.

(#553). "Good Morning." R. Atkinson Fox (printed). ©. K. Co--B.P. Co., N.Y. Even though this was issued as a separate and individual print, it should not have its own Fox-list number: "Good Morning" is the left-hand portion of #110 (Fig. 342, Book I), "Pleading at the Bar." 9 1/2 x 7 1/2. Courtesy Duane & Dolores Ramsey.

Fig. 339

Fig. 340

(#336). Untitled. R. Atkinson Fox. 8 1/4 x 12. Courtesy Loretta Goad.

(#431). "Fraternally Yours." 2613. R. Atkinson Fox. 20 x 15, 6 x 4. Courtesy JoAnn Mangskau.

Fig. 341

Fig. 342

129

(#446). Has also been found lithographed onto a metal serving tray advertising Strout Real Estate. 17 1/4 x 12 1/4. Courtesy Wm. C. & Becky Fox.

Fig. 343

Here is #431 on the cover of a 1935 catalog of farms for sale by the company. Courtesy Pat Gibson.

Fig. 343-a

(#417). Untitled. R. Atkinson Fox. 12 1/2 x 8 1/2. Courtesy Pat Gibson.

Fig. 344

(#335). "Spick and Span." R. Atkinson Fox. 12 x 9, 9 x 7. Ann Fox Mergenthaler collection. Photo by author.

Fig. 345

(#446). Untitled. R. Atkinson Fox. 10 1/2 x 7. Courtesy Pat Gibson.

Fig. 346

(#554). "At the Fountain." Painting by R.A. Fox. In this print, one horse is brown and one is white. It is an 11 x 8 oval. The print with the black horse is titled "A Well-earned Drink," Painting by R.A. Fox. ©. E.N. H-2433. It is printed as a 9 x 7 oval with an ornate mat. Courtesy Pat Gibson.

Fig. 347

(#464). "Friends." R. Atkinson Fox. ©. 1914, American Colortype Co., Chi. & N.Y. 20 x 16. Also found in 5 1/2 x 7, titled "Two Families." Courtesy Duane & Dolores Ramsey.

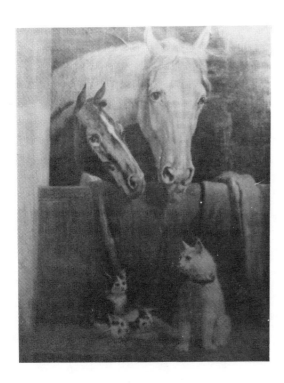

Fig. 348

(#511). "Pals." R. Atkinson Fox. ©. 1915. (Probably the one described in the L.C. list, pg. 143, Book I. The horses are virtually the same as #304 [Fig. 347, Book I], "At Your Service.") 8 x 6 1/2. Courtesy Pat Gibson.

Fig. 349

(#365). "Friendly Greeting." R. Atkinson Fox.©. H.P.W., Calendar top #1045. 15 x 12 1/2. Courtesy Ron & Bernie Shaw.

Fig. 350

(#584). Untitled. R.A... The right bottom corner of this print has been torn away taking most of the signature with it, but the "R" and "A" are very distinctive and easily recognized as RAF's. "Champion Harvesting Machines" appears at the top, and the International Harvester Logo is at left. 14 x 18, 21 x 15. Courtesy Barb Kratz.

Fig. 351

(#584). Also has been found as a 21 x 14 calendar advertising the Adrian (Michigan) Fair of Sept 20-24, 1915. ©. Hayes Litho Co., Buffalo, N.Y. This one is signed at lower left. Courtesy Ben & Sandra Ross.

Fig. 351-a

Here is a mirror image of #585 on the cover of a children's book titled "Beautiful Animals, ABC," ©. Charles E. Graham & Co., Newark, N.Y. & New York, 046, Holiday Series." Courtesy Barb Kratz.

Fig. 351-b

The puppies from #585 are found on an inside page of a children's book titled <u>Big Animal Book</u>, ©. Charles E. Graham & Co., Newark, N.J. and New York, 0427, Big Linen Series." Courtesy Barb Kratz.

The cover of the <u>Big Animal Book</u> that the puppies from #585 are found in is similar to the St. Bernard and children prints that we find signed "Colvin." Courtesy Barb Kratz.

A Family of Puppies

THESE puppies are the kind of dogs known by the name of Collies. These dogs are beautiful, also very intelligent. When grown up they are trained to watch and care for flocks of sheep. Collies are so kind and wise that they make fine playfellows for little children. Their silky coats are brown with a white breast.

Fig. 351-c

Fig. 351-d

(#647). Untitled. R. A. Fox. 8 x 12. Courtesy Lois & Jared Lange

(#698). "Who Said Dinner?" R. Atkinson Fox. Knapp Pub. Co. 1922 sample calendar. 9 x 12. Courtesy Margene & Terry Petros.

Fig. 352

Fig. 353

(#337). "Bred in the Purple." R. Atkinson Fox. Brown & Bigelow, St. Paul, U.S.A., 1914, #15080. 8 x 12, 5 1/2 x 8. Courtesy Ron & Deanna Hulse.

The left portion of #337 has been found, not titled or signed, in size 8 x 6 on a 1919 calendar for Brown & Bigelow. Courtesy Ruth & Dale Niemeier.

Fig. 354

Fig. 354-a

(#407). "After a Day's Work." #5511. Painting by Fox. © 1909 Gerlach Barklow Col, Joliet, Ill. This is a black & white print. 5 x 11. Courtesy Barb Kratz.

(#626). "The Day's Work Done." Fox. Title and artist are typeset. 11 x 8, 9 x 7. Courtesy Duane & Dolores Ramsey.

Fig. 355

Fig. 356

(#552). Untitled. R. Atkinson Fox. This print probably was wider because both the signature and one of the white horses have been partially cut off at right. 5 1/4 x 7 1/2. Also found on a blotter. Courtesy Ben & Sandra Ross.

Fig. 357

(#326). "Man and Beast Prepare the Land for the Sowing of the Grain." From painting by R.A. Fox. The K.T. Co., Cin., Ohio. Found on a 1918 calendar. 17 x 14. Courtesy Loretta Goad.

Fig. 358

(#344). "His First Lesson." R. Atkinson Fox. 9 1/2 x 7 1/2. On a 1927 adv. calendar. Courtesy Mary Battaglia.

Fig. 359

(#451). "Harvesting." Publisher's #4241. From painting by Fox. ©. 1908, The T.D.M. Co., Red Oak, Ia. (See Painting Record, pg. 44, Book I.) 1912 calendar. Print is 6 x 8. Courtesy Duane & Dolores Ramsey.

Fig. 360

(#362). "Going to the Fire." By R.A. Fox and J.A. Fraser (signed by RAF only). "1885" is under artists' names. From a March, 1946, magazine article. 13 1/2 x 9 1/2. Courtesy Ron & Bernie Shaw.

(#363). "Seeking Protection." R. Atkinson Fox. Publisher: R.A. Schneider, #1226. 9 x 7 1/2. Courtesy Ron & Bernie Shaw.

Fig. 361

(#645). "Fording the Stream." R. Atkinson Fox. 9 x 5. Courtesy Ben & Sandra Ross.

Fig. 363

Fig. 362

CATTLE

(#385). "The Emperor." R. Atkinson Fox. Portrait of a Hereford. 8 x 6. Courtesy Deanna Hulse

Fig. 364

(#696). "A Blue Ribbon Pair." From painting by R.A. Fox. ©. 1923, by Louis F. Dow Co. 12 x 18. Courtesy Margene & Terry Petros.

Fig. 365

(#655). Untitled. "Fox" as we are used to seeing it, with the top line of the "F" extending over the "ox," ©. 1910. 16 x 20. Courtesy Duane & Dolores Ramsey.

Fig. 366

(#654). "Peace and Contentment." W. Stewart, R. Atkinson Fox, and Painting by R. Atkinson Fox. What makes this print unusual is that fact that it has two signatures and an attribution. "W. Stewart" is the most apparent signature. "R. Atkinson Fox" appears, faintly, at lower right, and "Painting by Fox" is printed with the title and "2056" below the print. 10 1/2 x 7 5/8. Found on a 1915 calendar by Duane & Dolores Ramsey.

Fig. 367

(#619). Untitled. R. Atkinson Fox. ©. E.C. Cutler. 6 x 8 1/2. Courtesy Pat Gibson.

(#618). "High Noon." R. Atkinson Fox. K.T. Co., Cincinnati. 13 x 5. Courtesy Mary & Len Henning.

Fig. 368

Fig. 369

(#579). "At the Pool." sgnd. R.A. Fox & marked "Painting by R.A. Fox." ©. 1902, Brown & Bigelow, St. Paul. 7 1/2 x 10. Courtesy Pat Gibson.

(#578). In the Meadow Pasture. R. Atkinson Fox. 9 x 12. Courtesy Pat Gibson

Fig. 370

Fig. 371

139

(#556). Untitled. R.A. Fox. ©. 1902, Chas. Ehler, Cincinnati. 1923 sample calendar. 7 x 11. Courtesy Duane & Dolores Ramsey.

(#502). "Returning From Pasture." ©. 1918 by Chas. Williams, N.Y., #109. R. Atkinson Fox. 9 x 7, 14 x 10. Courtesy Ben & Sandra Ross.

Fig. 372

Fig. 373

(#498). Untitled. 8 1/4 x 11 1/2. Courtesy Duane & Dolores Ramsey.

(#479). "Prize Stock." From painting by R. Atkinson Fox. 8 x 10. Courtesy Barb Kratz.

Fig. 374

Fig. 375

(#474). "Bonnie J. International Champion." R. Atkinson Fox. Below image is printed: "Hereford/ Origin: England. Color: red with white markings, including head. Weigh 1300 to 2300 lbs. Popular range animal. Thrive under adverse conditions. Thrive in the South and on the plains as well as in the Corn Belt. Mature early. Easily fattened." 3 1/2 x 5. Courtesy Duane & Dolores Ramsey.

Fig. 376

(#472). "Prize Winners." R. Atkinson Fox. Below image is printed: "Shorthorn / Origin: England and Scotland. Color: red, roan and white. The largest breed of cattle, many of them weighing as much as 2500 lbs. Popular in all parts of America and Canada for cross-breeding and grading up. They mature early." 3 1/2 x 5. Courtesy Duane & Dolores Ramsey

Fig. 377

(#458). "Contentment." R. Atkinson Fox. A painting with this title sold at the Leonard Auction in Boston in 1893. (See pg. 27, Book I.) 5 x 7, 7 x 10. Courtesy Ben & Sandra Ross.

Fig. 378

(#460). "Monarchs of the Prairie." R. Atkinson Fox. © 1908 by Chas. Williams, N.Y. 7 x 10. Courtesy Wm. C. & Becky Fox.

Fig. 379

(#452). "The Pasture Lane." Artist, Fox (verified). Found on a 1911 calendar. Print, 15 x 5. Courtesy Pat Gibson.

Fig. 380

(#435). "Prosperity." R.A. Fox. 7 x 9 Courtesy Milan Royle.

Fig. 381

(#453). "The Watering Place." R.A. Fox. ©. W.H. Carpenter. 5 x 7 print. This has also been found on two postacrds: One is marked, ©. R. Hill; the other is from "Art Series No. 276, American News Co., N.Y. & Leipzig, Dresden." This latter one has "Greetings from Corinth N.Y." in glitter across the front. Courtesy Ben Sandra Ross.

Fig. 382

(#353). "When Evening Calls Them Home." R. Atkinson Fox. Found on a 1923 calendar by Stan Noreika.

Fig. 383

(#359). "On the Meadows." R. Atkinson Fox. 6 1/2 x 10. Courtesy Wm. C. & Becky Fox.

(#369). "Shorthorns Nooning." R. Atkinson Fox. The Osborne Co., Newark, N.J. and Toronto, Ontario. 9 1/2 x 13 1/2. Also found on a signed, 11 x 16, 300-piece, "Warren Built-Rite" puzzle made by Warren Paper Products Co., Lafayette, Indiana. Courtesy Ron & Bernie Shaw.

Fig. 384

Fig. 385

(#403). "As the Sun Goes Down." R. Atkinson Fox. 11 x 14. Courtesy Barb Kratz.

"As the Sun Goes Down" has also been found on a 7 x 5 advertising thermometer. Author's collection.

Fig. 386

Fig. 386-a

143

(#404). "By Winding Stream." R.A. Fox. 1901, C.R. Gibson & Co., 7626-7-25. Here are two of the three cows from #403, "As the Sun Goes Down." The colors and backgrounds are different, but these two cows are the same! And they are not by the stream, they are in it. Also found on a postcard, as a 6 1/4 x 9 1/2, black & white print, and as a 5 x 7 print with advertising. Courtesy Maryhelen Koeberl.

Fig. 387

(#408). "In the Pasture Stream." From painting by Fox. Presented to a student by a teacher in 1905. 5 1/4 x 7 1/4. Courtesy Barb Kratz.

Fig. 388

(#415). "Prize Winners." R. Atkinson Fox. Publisher's #9778. Autumn colors. 8 x 10. Courtesy Wm. C. & Becky Fox.

Fig. 389

(#580). "Short Horns." From painting by Fox, M-2121. © 1909, TDM Co., Red Oak, Ia. 5 1/2 x 10 1/2. Courtesy Duane & Dolores Ramsey.

Fig. 390

(#704). "Peaceful Valley." R. Atkinson Fox. ©. 1914, Brown Shoe Co., St. Louis. #532 has the same title. The print is 7 1/8 x 5 1/4, & the overall calendar measures 12 3/4 x 8 1/8. Courtesy Margene & Terry Petros.

#704 is found as a "Buster Brown" advertising piece with a 1916 calendar pad. Petros.

Fig. 391

Fig. 391-a

145

(#430). "In the Pasture." Publisher's #4550. Also titled, "A Proud Mother." Publisher's #4326. Signed R.A. Fox, and attributed to H. Musson in a 1903 Thos. D. Murphy Co. catalog. (Also see Painting Record #77, pg. 43, Book I.) This is one of the few pseudonyms on the Fox list. That's because it was found with the sig. R. Atkinson Fox and listed before it was found with the Musson reference. Sizes listed on the painting record are 8 x 6 1/2 and 10 1/4 x 8 1/4. Each size has a different series number and was produced by a different company. Courtesy Barb Kratz.

Fig. 392

(#730). "The Herefords." From Painting by Fox. ©. 1908, TDM Co., Red Oak, Ia. (Also on P.A.P. list.) This is the combined print--we had previously listed a right-side portion as #386, and the left side as #646. Found on a 1910 calendar by Pat Gibson.
The following has been found on the back of one portion:
"In this painting the artist, Mr. Fox, used as a model a prize herd of Herefords that was formerly owned on a ranch near Ashland, Nebraska. The stock farm has now passed out of existence, but in its day it was considered the home of the finest cattle in the United States. The man who owned it frequently paid thousands of dollars for a single animal, and his breed of Herefords was called superior to anything then known, taking prizes in livestock shows in all parts of the country. Mr. Fox has risen grandly to his opportunities in this instance, for each individual steer will bear the closest sort of inspection, so accurately has he painted them. To do the herd of white-faced beauties, he has added a landscape effect which cannot help but please the most exacting critic.
R. Atkinson Fox is a clever American artist, who makes his home in Philadelphia and whose power lies in his ability to give an air of absolute naturalness to his pictures and in his carefulness to detail. His work is highly esteemed, both by connoisseurs of art and by the public in general. During the last few years, he has retired from active work and anything from his brush is now exceedingly hard to obtain."
On page 42 of Book I, I show a painting record from the Thos. D. Murphy Co. for a painting titled "Herefords." I'm not sure this is the same one as the description seems somewhat different. However, it does mention the "boy on horseback in rear."

Fig. 393

(#471). "Herefords." Publisher's #4244. ©. T.D.M. Co., Red Oak, Ia. Described in Painting Record on pg. 44, Book I, as "Eight Hereford cattle lined up in a row, looking." 1912 calendar sample. Three sizes are listed: 6 x 8, 12 x 16 & 8 x 16. Courtesy Duane & Dolores Ramsey.

Fig. 394

(#705). Untitled. R.A. Fox. No publisher info. Four Jerseys lined up for a group picture. 6 x 8. Courtesy Margene & Terry Petros.

Fig. 395

(#764). "Jerseys." Identified as RAF by People's Art Project. Thos. D. Murphy Co. Courtesy People's Art Project, and JII/Sales Promotion Associates, Red Oak, Iowa.

Fig. 396

(#462). Untitled. R. Atkinson Fox. 5 x 7. Courtesy Duane & Dolores Ramsey.

Fig. 397

(#697). Untitled. R. Atkinson Fox. 8 1/4 x 6 1/8. Courtesy Ben & Sandra Ross.

Fig. 398

(#540). "The Close of Day." R.A. Fox. ©. 1902, R.E. Maskin, Chi. On the front and back is advertising for 1904 calendars. One noteworthy line states: "Beautiful color work from paintings--not photographs--worth several thousand dollars." 8 1/4 x 6 1/4. Courtesy Pat Gibson.

Fig. 399

(#483). "Country Road." R.A. Fox. 5 x 7. Courtesy Pat Gibson.

Fig. 400

(#691). "Evening--4319." sgnd. R.A. Fox. Attributed to H. Musson. ©. 1902, TDM Co. Described on Painting Record #74, pg. 43, Book I. Photographed from TDM Co. catalog. Courtesy Barb Kratz.

Fig. 401

148

(#555). "Chewing the Cud." R. Atkinson Fox. ©. 1913, R. Hill. This scene may have been wider as the signature is slightly cut off on the right. 5 3/4 x 7 1/4. Courtesy Duane & Dolores Ramsey.

Fig. 402

(#539). "Thoroughbreds." R. Atkinson Fox. ©. American Lithographic Co., 1902. 10 x 16. Courtesy Pat Gibson.

Fig. 403

(#536). Untitled. R.A. Fox. Courtesy Pat Gibson.

Fig. 404

(#507). "Browsing." R. Atkinson Fox. ©. 1904, R. Hill. 6 x 8. Courtesy Pat Gibson.

Fig. 405

149

(#473). "Aberdeen Angus." R. Atkinson Fox. Below image is printed: "Aberdeen Angus/Origin: Scotland. Solid black in color. No horns. Weigh from 1600 up to 2100 lbs. Hardy and good rustlers. Early maturing. Fatten rapidly. Thrive in Gulf States and Northern Canada as well as in the Middle West." 3 1/2 x 5. Courtesy Duane & Dolores Ramsey.

ABERDEEN ANGUS
Origin: Scotland. Solid black in color. No horns. Weigh from 1600 up to 2100 lbs. Hardy and good rustlers. Early maturing. Fatten rapidly. Thrive in Gulf States and Northern Canada as well as in the Middle West.

Fig. 406

(#455). "Woodland and Cattle." R.A. Fox. The Art Interchange Co., N.Y. 16 x 13 1/2. Courtesy Ron & Clare Santelli.

Fig. 407

(#454). "Champions of the West." R.A. Fox. ©. 1909, Chas. Williams, N.Y. Hereford bull in front is the same as #120 (Fig 313, Book I). The backgrounds are different. 8 x 11. Courtesy Pat Gibson.

Fig. 408

(#434). Untitled. R. Atkinson Fox. 12 x 9. Courtesy Della Simmons.

Fig. 409

(#406). "A Summer Day." R. Atkinson Fox. ©. 1903 by J.W. Crane. From a painting by R. Atkinson Fox. The Osborne Co., N.Y. 1904 calendar. 7 x 10 1/2. Courtesy Barb Kratz.

(#672). "Scotch Shorthorns... D.E. Lomas Farm, Villisca, Ia." Not signed. Identified in Thos. D. Murphy book and on P.A.P. list for 1925. 12 x 16. Courtesy Pat Gibson.

Fig. 410

Fig. 411

(#427). "U.S.A. Quality." R. Atkinson Fox. 8 x 10. Courtesy Pat Gibson.

(#617). "A Bunch of Beauties." R. Atkinson Fox. 8 x 10. Courtesy Pat Gibson.

Fig. 412

Fig. 413

151

(#529). "A Peaceful Day." R. Atkinson Fox. 6 x 4, 8 x 10. Courtesy Pat Gibson.

Fig. 414

(#729). "Getting Together." Attributed to RAF in Red Wing Paintings Book. The oil is listed as 16 x 36 and $40. Print is 5 x 15. Courtesy Margene & Terry Petros.

Fig. 415

(#648). "Future Prize Winners." By R.A. Fox. The Lutz Calendar Co., Burlington, Ia. No. 992, ©. 1902. 7 1/2 x 10 1/2. Courtesy Pat Gibson.

Fig. 416

(#497). Untitled. R. Atkinson Fox. 8 1/2 x 12 1/2. Courtesy Duane & Dolores Ramsey.

Fig. 417

(#521). "The Three Twins." Publisher's #3016. R.A. Fox. ©. 1909, Gerlach-Barklow Co., Joliet, Ill. 4 x 10. Courtesy Ben & Sandra Ross.

(#426). "Prides of the West." R. Atkinson Fox. 8 x 11. Courtesy Pat Gibson.

Fig. 418

(#480). "Top Notchers." R. Atkinson Fox. 6 x 8. Courtesy Barb Kratz.

Fig. 419

Fig. 420

153

DOGS

(#586). "Hero of the Alps." R. Atkinson Fox. ©. 1909 by Chas. Williams, N.Y. 8 x 6. Courtesy Wm. C. & Becky Fox.

(#510). Untitled. R. Atkinson Fox. ©. Campbell Art Co. 7 1/2 x 9 1/2. Courtesy Jerre Jones.

Fig. 421

Fig. 422

(#615). "Juleposten I Nordlandet." Efter Maleri av Robert Atkinson Fox. Jul i Vesterheimen, 1938. 12 x 9. Also reported on an 8 x 6, 1933 calendar titled "Winter's Trail." Courtesy Pat Gibson.

(#478). "The Open Season." R. Atkinson Fox. 6 x 8. Courtesy Barb Kratz.

Fig. 423

Fig. 424

155

(#649). "The Pointer." R. Atkinson Fox. 12 x 8. Ann Fox Mergenthaler collection. Photo by author.

Fig. 425

(#726). "Thrills Afield." Attributed to RAF in Red Wing Paintings Book. Oil is listed as 33 3/8 x 26 1/2 and $75. Print is 9 1/2 x 6 1/2. Courtesy Margene & Terry Petros.

Fig. 426

(#587). "The Three Pals." From painting by R.A. Fox. ©. K.T. Co., Cin., Ohio. "There's a Joy that Thrills in the Sport that Fills\The Golden Days of the Hunt." 9 x 12. Courtesy Barb Kratz.

Fig. 427

(#357). "A Tense Moment." Painting by Fox. Courtesy Clare Cerda.

Fig. 428

(#441). "With Dog & Gun." R.A. Fox. ©. 1907 by Fred C. Lounsbury. 5 x 7. Courtesy Barbara Kern.

Fig. 429

(#713). "October Sport." This print is unsigned. See LC list, Book I: Same title, ©. R.A. Fox, Aug. 11, 1905, I-15163. This is a Jig-a-Jig, J-25 wooden puzzle by Parker Bros. It is copyrighted by Chas. Williams, N.Y. Notice that this is the same man as #441--the dog & background are different. 5 7/8 x 7 7/8. Courtesy Wm. C. & Becky Fox.

(#550). "In Full Chase." R.A. Fox. (7815) ©. H. McCauley. Here is the "Fox Hunt" by RAF himself! Five hounds leap over a fallen tree "in full chase" of a frightened red fox. 5 1/2 x 8. Courtesy Pat Gibson.

Fig. 430

Fig. 431

157

(#437). "In Full Cry." R. Atkinson Fox. Courtesy Lois Trimble.

Fig. 432

(#667). "A Reliable Guardian." R. Atkinson Fox. Publisher's #4501. 9 x 12 and 15 7/8 x 20 on a 1927 calendar. Courtesy Nick Morin.

Fig. 433

(#588). "On Guard." From painting by R.A. Fox. ©. E.N. H-2435. 11 x 8. Courtesy Pat Gibson.

Fig. 436

(#370). "Rover." From a painting by R.A. Fox. E.N. #2155. The Fox family dog is featured against a background of mountains. From a 1922 calendar. 5 x 7 1/2. Courtesy Ron & Bernie Shaw.

Fig. 437

(#346). "On the Alert." R. Atkinson Fox. Publisher's #2131, The American Art Works, Coshocton, Ohio. 8 x 12. Courtesy Donna Robinson.

(#725). "Vigilance." Attributed to RAF in Red Wing Paintings Book. The oil is listed as 30 x 24 & was listed at $100. The print is 11 1/2 x 10. Other prints measure 9 x 7 & 8 x 6. Courtesy Margene & Terry Petros.

Fig. 438

Fig. 439

(#589). "The Anxious Mother." Signed R. Atkinson. With the period. There's plenty of room for "Fox" had he wanted to put it there. He must have just been experimenting with a variation of his own name. ©. 1907 by Fred C. Lounsbury. 1909 calendar. 10 x 4. Courtesy Ben & Sandra Ross.

(#484). "Waiting for Their Master." R. Atkinson Fox. Also, © 1905, by R. Atkinson Fox; and From Painting by R. Atkinson Fox. Publisher's #4416, The Osborne Co., N.Y. (See L.C. listing, pg. 143, Book I.) Courtesy Ben & Sandra Ross.

Fig. 441

"Waiting for Their Master" was first found as the bottom insert of an old clock. Courtesy Wm. C. & Becky Fox.

Fig. 440

Fig. 442

MISCELLANEOUS ANIMALS

(#699). "The Challenge." (Identified as RAF from "People's Art Project" list.) 14 x 21. Courtesy Ben & Sandra Ross.

Fig. 443

(#442). "The Monarchs." Painting by R.A. Fox. Found on a 1917 calendar. 6 x 8. Courtesy Pat Gibson. Also found on a 1927 sample calendar titled "In the Pride of Their Strength."

Fig. 444

(#614). "Supreme." From painting by R.A. Fox. 8 1/2 x 12. Ann Fox Mergenthaler Collection. Photo by author.

Fig. 445

(#613). "Monarch of the North." R. Atkinson Fox. M.P. Co. 14 1/2 x 10. Courtesy Pat Gibson.

Fig. 446

(#421). Untitled. R. Atkinson Fox. 10 x 8. Courtesy Barb Kratz.

Fig. 447

(#516). Untitled. R. Atkinson Fox. 14 x 12. Courtesy Pat Gibson. This has also been found on a 1915 sample calendar, titled, and marked "Hayes Litho. Co., Buffalo, N.Y." In this 1915 calendar print, only half the bear is visible, and there are more mountains, more sky, and less stream.

Fig. 448

(#763). "A Native Son." Identified as RAF by People's Art Project. Thos. D. Murphy Co. Courtesy People's Art Project, and JII/Sales Promotion Associates, Red Oak, Iowa.

Fig. 449

(#576). "The Sentinel." R. Atkinson Fox. ©. 1910 by Chas. Williams, N.Y. It's as if the viewer is in a cave looking out at this bear. The bear (identical to the one in #373) is looking out over a canyon where the sun is setting in the bkgrnd. Found on a 1912 calendar. 6 x 8. Courtesy Pat Gibson.

Fig. 450

(#373). "The Sentry." R. Atkinson Fox. Frederickson Co., Chicago. 16 x 12. Courtesy Wm. C. & Becky Fox.

A portion of #373--just the bear on the cliff with the waterfall in the background--appears on the cover of a child's booklet titled "In the Jungle," published by American Colortype Co., Chicago. A wider, but still incomplete, portion of the same print appears inside the book with the title, "Old Bruin." Courtesy Ben & Sandra Ross.

Fig. 451

Fig. 452

(#653). "An Uninvited Guest...And like the bee, stole all the sweets away." Painting by Fox. ©. Baumgarth, Chicago. 5 1/2 x 4. 1921 calendar. Courtesy Duane & Dolores Ramsey.

(#549). "Fury of the Flames." R. Atkinson Fox. 8 x 12. Courtesy Duane & Dolores Ramsey.

Fig. 453

Fig. 454

(#676). "The Kingdom of the Wild." R. Atkinson Fox. ©. 1912, A.M. Collins Mfg. Co. Found on a 1914 salesman's sample calendar. Image is 6 x 8 3/8. Courtesy Ben & Sandra Ross.

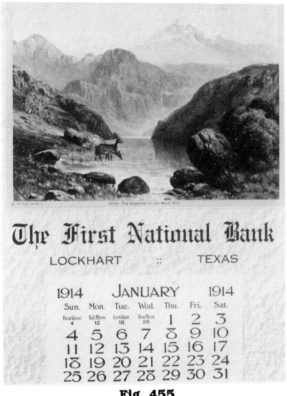

The First National Bank

LOCKHART :: TEXAS

1914   JANUARY   1914

Sun.	Mon.	Tue.	Wed.	Thu.	Fri.	Sat.
First Quar. 4	Full Moon 12	Last Quar. 18	New Moon 26	1	2	3
4	5	6	7	8	9	10
11	12	13	14	15	16	17
18	19	20	21	22	23	24
25	26	27	28	29	30	31

Fig. 455

(#381). "Evening in the Mountains." R. Atkinson Fox. The American Art Works, Coshocton, Ohio. Moose at left emerging from the water and walking toward another moose on the right shore. Courtesy Donna Eby.

Fig. 456

(#481). "The Morning Call." R. Atkinson Fox. 8 x 12. Courtesy Barb Kratz.

Fig. 457

(#735). "The Night Call." Label on back: "H-139, 'The Night Call,' Fox." This is pretty skimpy attribution. The backing with the label does appear to be original. This is the same elk found in #481 and #509. And the title seems to make it a match with #481. 9 x 13. Courtesy Hugh Hetzer.

Fig. 458

165

(#509). "The Challenge." (R. Atkinson Fox). Thos. D. Murphy Co. Here is the exact same elk from #481 and #735 pictured on a blotter. The fact that the elk are the same and that "The Challenge" is listed in the L.C. listing on pg. 141 of Book I, seems documentation enough. 3 1/2 x 3 1/4. Courtesy Barb Kratz.

Fig. 459

"The Answering Call." Unsigned. Here, one more time, is that same elk seen in #481, #509, and #735, with still a different background. This one doesn't have a Fox list number because nothing has been found to indicate that it is a Fox--other than the identical rendering of the elk, of course. 8 x 12. Courtesy Ben & Sandra Ross.

Fig. 460

(#514). "The Monarch of the North." Artist: Fox. © 1914, Red Wing Adv. Co. 15 x 5, 9 x 7. Courtesy Duane & Dolores Ramsey.

Fig. 461

(#515). "Sunset in the Big North Woods." Painting by R. Atkinson Fox. © F.A.S. Publisher's #4053. 10 1/2 x 11. Courtesy Duane & Dolores Ramsey.

Fig. 462

(#728). "The Monarch." Attributed to RAF in Red Wing Paintings Book. The oil is sized as 15 7/8 x 20 & listed at $100. Print is 10 1/2 x 10. Courtesy Margene & Terry Petros.

"The Monarch" is also found facing the title page in an art book titled <u>Jul i Vesterheimen</u> (see also, Fig. 423). I have been told this refers to "A Western Christmas," and there is a museum by that name in Decorah, Iowa. The book was published by Augsburg Publishing House, Minneapolis, Minn. Courtesy Nick Morin.

Fig. 463

Fig. 463-a

(#677). "The Call." R. Atkinson Fox. ©. 1912 by E.C. Cutler. ©. 1912, A.M. Collins Mfg., Co. This print is described in the Library of Congress (LC) listing that starts on pg. 141 of Book I. Two examples are found--one with" 3619, The Call--Fox" and one with "3527." The 3619 does not carry the E.C. Cutler copyright. Found on a 1914 salesman's sample calendar. Image is 7 x 11. Courtesy Ben & Sandra Ross.

(#527). "The Last of the Herd." Painting by R. Atkinson Fox. 8 1/2 x 12 1/2. Courtesy Pat Gibson.

Fig. 464

Fig. 465

The following was found on the back of a 1913, salesman's sample calendar of #527. Courtesy Ben & Sandra Ross.

Fig. 465-a

(#650). "Startled." R. Atkinson Fox. 6 x 12. Ann Fox Mergenthaler collection. Photo by author.

Fig. 466

(#461). "Wild Life." R. Atkinson Fox. 9 x 6. Courtesy Duane & Dolores Ramsey.

Fig. 467

(#348). "Northward Bound." R. Atkinson Fox. ©. T.D.M. Co., Red Oak, Ia. 12 1/2 x 8 1/2. According to Painting Record #1174 (pg. 44, Book One), the author's title for this painting was "Duck Shooting." Ann Fox Mergenthaler collection. Photo by author.

Fig. 468

(#689). Untitled. R.A. Fox. 15 x 5. Courtesy Pat Gibson.

Fig. 469

(#695). "America's Breadbasket." Unsigned. Thos. D. Murphy Co., Red Oak, Ia. See LC listing, pg. 141, Book I. This is also on the "People's Art Project" list. Very similar to #690. 16 x 22 1/2. Courtesy Margene & Terry Petros.

Fig. 470

(#690). "After the Harvest--4314." No signature. Attributed to H. Musson. ©. 1902, TDM Co. See Painting Record, bottom left corner, pg. 43, Book I: "Wheat Field in shocks. Chickens in foreground. Blue sky." This painting record was the first indication we had of Musson as a pseudonym. The painting record indicates the original was "destroyed." Photographed from a TDM Co. catalog by Barb Kratz.

Fig. 471

(#727). Untitled. R. Atkinson Fox. Beautiful red parrots (Scarlet Macaws?) on a marble terrace overlooking blue water, trees & mountains. 11 1/2 x 9. Courtesy Mark & Carol Graham.

Fig. 472

(#433). "The Leader." Publisher's #4219. Painting by R. Atkinson Fox. ©. F.A.S. 11 x 10. Courtesy Pat Gibson. A mirror-image of this print has been found signed "Chs. Stacey." (See "Possible Pseudonyms & Other Confusing Signatures.")

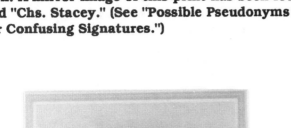

Fig. 473

(#532). "Peaceful Valley." Painting by R. Atkinson Fox. 8 x 11. Courtesy Pat Gibson.

Fig. 474

(#340). "Safely Guarded." R. Atkinson Fox. Lutz & Gould Co., Burlington, Ia. Found on a 1901 calendar by Cecilia Shull.

Fig. 475

Here is a closer look at the sheep in "Safely Guarded."

Fig. 475-a

170

(#334). Untitled. R.A. Fox. © C.D.W. Stern & Co., Inc., Phila. 8 x 20. Courtesy Tim Wrobel.

(#692). "Homeward Bound--4316." Sgnd. R.A. Fox. Attributed to H. Musson. © 1902, TDM Co. Check Painting Record #515, pg. 44, Book I. Photographed from a TDM Co. catalog by Barb Kratz.

Fig. 476

Fig. 477

(#620). "Old Faithful." R. Atkinson Fox. Louis F. Dow. "Old Faithful" must refer to the dog that is herding this small flock of sheep over a muddy path. 13 x 18. Courtesy Ruth & Dale Niemeier.

Fig. 478

(#577). "In Green Pastures." R.A. Fox. The Beckwith Co., Norwich, Conn. No. 865. ©. 1903 by L.C. Co. 6 x 8. Courtesy Pat Gibson.

Fig. 479

(#762). "Purebred Herd." Identified as RAF by People's Art Project. Thos. D. Murphy Co. Courtesy People's Art Project, and JII/Sales Promotion Associates, Red Oak, Iowa.

Fig. 480

GARNET BANCROFT (G.B.) FOX

Garnet Bancroft (G.B.) Fox

Garnet Fox has remained somewhat elusive. According to family members, he never married or had children of his own; instead he traveled, worked when he wanted or needed to, and more or less drifted in and out of their lives. We do know that he must have been born about 1891--a drawing in his scrapbook has him at age nine in the year 1900.

A number of his prints have surfaced, however, and they are collected by many Fox admirers--although not with the fervor reserved for the works of RAF. Nonetheless--and despite the obvious influence and assistance of his uncle--Garnet's work exhibits a fine talent and deserves admiration in its own right.

Garnet kept a scrapbook which has been carefully preserved by one of RAF's daughters. She graciously allowed me to photograph it. The contents were as revealing as some of the female sketches. In addition to the mementoes of his youth and the normal kinds of things one might expect to find in a scrapbook, it is apparent that Garnet kept up with politics and news of the Royal Family--possibly a necessary part of his work as a politics cartoonist. World War I, of course, is a dominant theme through much of the scrapbook.

I have chosen a few items of interest that I hope will communicate the flavor of the scrapbook and something of the personality of the artist. What appears here represents only a small fraction of the published cartoons, clippings, sketches and other work contained in the book.

(Note: As pointed out in Book I, Garnet often used the pseudonym, "Guy Fawkes" or "G. Fawkes" because he apparently enjoyed the similarity between his name and that of the famous conspirator who was executed in England in 1605.)

Garnet's interest in art apparently started early. A small drawing of a ship is marked "Garnet Fox, age 9, Jan. 4th, 1900."

Another early occupies a corner of one page. This small painting depicts a youthful (Scottish?) soldier and is inscribed "Garnet--age 11 years," and labeled "My first oil painting." Admirers of Garnet's dog prints will also recognize the inspiration for some of his paintings on this page.

Fig. 481

Fig. 482

In addition to the inspiration he obviously received from his "Uncle Bob," Garnets artistic efforts must have been encouraged by his father as well. A rough drawing labeled "Sketch by my Dad of Indian near Esquimaux [Eskimo] country in Hudson Bay" was a treasure to be preserved.

Another reference to Garnet's father is contained in the label of a faded, stained black-and-white photo of a distant ship amid ice floes. It reads, "Dad's ship 'Neptune' in Artic."

Fig. 483

Fig. 484

A number of poems and song lyrics earned a place in Garnet's scrapbook. Among them, the poem "Hymn Before Action," by Rudyard Kipling. At the bottom right of this page is what appears to be a promotional piece Garnet did for the British Navy. It is signed "G. Fox."

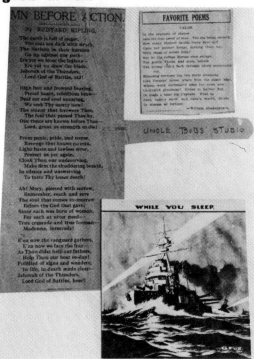

Fig. 485

Another "promotional" piece? This is signed "G. Fox, H.M.T. Willonyx."

Fig. 486

Garnet's time in the Navy is marked by his sketch of a shipmate, "Royal Hedges, Tenth Cruiser Squadron."

Fig. 487

Below this drawing of "The Shipyard," is a comic self-portrait. The caption reads "Commodore Fox in his office maturing plans for the largest warship ever built."

Fig. 488

This page is captioned, "Some practice heads when I thought I might try fashion work. Big flop."

Fig. 489

Garnet apparently did a series of cartoons for the "Toronto Sunday World," titled "Do You Realize..." The one with the coal bin is signed "G. Fox." The others are signed "G. Fawkes" and dated 1921.

Fig. 490

Fig. 491

Fig. 492

177

Another small oil painting with a "military" theme is undated and signed "G. Fawkes." It exhibits an interesting treatment of clouds and sun-brightened mountain tops. The plane is vividly painted in white, navy blue and red.

Here are a couple of selections to illustrate Garnet's talent as a political cartoonist. "The Spendthrift" is signed "G. Fox." The Taxpayer/Government cartoon is signed "G. Fawkes" and dated 1921.

Fig. 493

Fig. 494

Fig. 495

"Majestic Nature." G.B. Fox. 10 x 8. Courtesy Pat Gibson.

"Majestic Nature." G.B. Fox. Found on a titled, signed "Quality Picture Puzzle," by Ben & Sandra Ross.

Fig. 496

Fig. 496-a

"The Mountain Stream." G.B. Fox. No. J-204. © CHN. Has been found as a 17 x 22 print on a large, sample calendar, and as 8 x 6 and 10 x 8 portions. Courtesy John Jeagers.

Untitled. G.B. Fox. Morris & Bendien Inc., N.Y. 18 x 22. Courtesy Pat Gibson.

Fig. 497

Fig. 498

Untitled. G.B. Fawkes. Found on a 1940 calendar by Margene & Terry Petros.

Fig. 499

Untitled. G. Bancroft Fawkes. This is the cover of the October, 1937 issue of a German-American Magazine whose title means "The Housewife." It was published in Milwaukee, Wis. Courtesy Wm. C. & Becky Fox.

Fig. 500

"Meadowbrook." G. Bancroft Fox. 9 1/2 x 7. Courtesy Pat Gibson.

Fig. 501

"Sentinels of the Lake." G.B. Fox. 9 x 7. Courtesy Della Simmons.

Fig. 502

"The Great Outdoors." G.B. Fox. 10 x 8. Courtesy Pat Gibson.

Fig. 503

Untitled. G.B. Fox. A family of three deer is on the left bank at midground. 8 x 10. Courtesy Wm. C. & Becky Fox.

Fig. 504

"Protected." G.B. Fox. 9 x 7. Courtesy Pat Gibson.

Fig. 505

"Monarch of the North." G.B. Fox. 9 x 7. Courtesy Pat Gibson.

Fig. 506

"When Seconds Count." (Also found with title "Big Moment.") G. Bancroft. 12 x 9, 7 x 8. Courtesy Pat Gibson.

Fig. 507

Untitled. G. Bancroft. (This signature is at the lower right, so it could be cut off.) You might have to look closely to see the second moose on the opposite bank. Courtesy Margene & Terry Petros.

Fig. 508

"Out Where the West Begins." G.B. Fox. 9 1/2 x 7. Courtesy Pat Gibson.

Fig. 509

"Tranquility." G. Fawkes. ©. FMT. Joliet, Il. 10 1/4 x 8 1/2. Collection Ann Fox Mergenthaler. Photo by author.

Fig. 510

"The House by the Side of the Road." G.B. Fox. 9 x 12. Found on a 1938 calendar by Pat Gibson.

"Lovely as a Dream of June Time." Painting by G.B. Fox. You might not be able to see the dog lying in the path in front of the house. 9 x 12. Courtesy Pat Gibson.

Fig. 511

Fig. 512

"So Sweet the Dreams, So Pure the Thought/Of Home Sweet Home Which Love Hath Wrought. G. Fox. 9 x 12. Courtesy Pat Gibson.

Untitled. You might not be able to see the cows in the water to the right of the covered bridge. 9 x 7. Courtesy Pat Gibson.

Fig. 513

Fig. 514

"Where Dreams Come True." G.B. Fox. 10 x 13, 7 x 9. Also found as an advertising thermometer. Courtesy Pat Gibson.

Fig. 515

"The Old Mill." G.B. Fox. Found as a small, 5 x 4 print, and this 15 x 11 puzzle. Courtesy Ben & Sandra Ross.

Fig. 516

"Golden & Sunny & Filled With Good Cheer/A Home of Our Own, to Our Hearts Always Dear." Found with signatures, G.B. Fox and Garner Fox. ©. The Kemper Thomas Co., Cin. 9 x 11 3/4, 16 x 20. Courtesy Lois & Jared Lange.

Fig. 517

Untitled. G.B. Fox. K.T. Co., Cin., Ohio. U.S.A. This has been found as prints in 15 1/2 x 21 1/2 and 7 x 9, as well as the advertising thermometer pictured. Courtesy Margene & Terry Petros.

Fig. 518

Untitled. G.B. Fox. 8 x 10. Found as an advertising thermometer by Ben & Sandra Ross.

"A Home of Happy Memories." G. Fawkes. 9 3/8 x 7. Courtesy Ben & Sandra Ross.

Fig. 519

Fig. 520

"A Strike." G. Bancroft. (Signature is not cut off.) "Pict. No. 15" is printed at lower right. 9 x 7. Courtesy Pat Gibson.

"Sunset in the North Woods." G. Bancroft. (Signature is not cut off.) 10 x 8. Courtesy Ben & Sandra Ross.

Fig. 521

Fig. 522

"A Favorite Spot." G.B. Fox. ©. FMT, Joliet, Il. "779" is printed at lower left. This has been found on a 1934 calendar. 9 1/2 x 7 1/2. Collection Ann Fox Mergenthaler. Photo by author.

"At the Close of Day." G.B. Fox. Some examples show slightly more at left, but cut off the tallest tree. 10 x 8, 8 x 6. Also found on a 16 x 20 Tuco Puzzle. Photo by author.

Fig. 523

Fig. 524

Untitled. G.B. Fox. This ad appeared on a 1936 calendar. 22 x 14. Courtesy Hugh Hetzer.

"Dream Garden." G. Bancroft. Signature is at lower right and could be cut off. 9 x 6 1/2. Courtesy Pat Gibson.

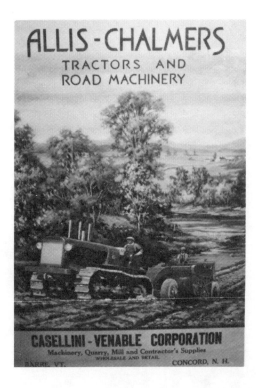

Fig. 525

Fig. 526

Untitled. G. Bancroft Fox. 7 x 5.

Fig. 527

"The Enchanted Pool." G. Bancroft Fox. Garnet must have liked redheads dressed in yellow. That description fits this picture as well as the next one, "A Pair of Beauties." And they could both be the same young woman. 12 x 10. Courtesy Pat Gibson.

Fig. 528

"A Pair of Beauties." G.B. Fox. 9 1/2 x 7. Also found on a fan. Courtesy Pat Gibson.

Fig. 529

"Little Gardener." G.B. Fox. Publisher's #522. O.H.K. Found on a 9 x 7 print and this art deco fan. Courtesy Lois & Jared Lange.

Fig. 530

Untitled. G.B. Fox. Cover of Apr. 20, 1903 issue of "Leslie's Weekly" magazine. Actually, this presents a problem. According to Garnet's scrapbook, he was nine in 1900. That makes him only 12 when this was published. The signature is at lower left, below the girl's dress. 11 x 9. Gibson.

Fig. 531

"Tom, Dick and Harry." G.B. Fox, signed in elaborate calligraphy. 9 1/2 x 7 3/4. Courtesy Barb Kratz.

Fig. 532

"Faithful to his Trust." The signature reportedly looks like "Garnet <u>W.</u> Fox." It is not written like any of Garnet's normal signatures, and the "Fox" looks more like RAF's signature. 7 x 12. Courtesy Pat Gibson.

Fig. 533

"What Price Pal?" Unsigned. This is from Garnet's scrapbook. It was on a page with two other of his published prints. This has been found, also unsigned, with a more vertical orientation--the boys legs and feet can be seen at the bottom and a "Pet Shop" sign is above. Note also #811, "Puppies for Sale," on the Brown & Bigelow list, page 38, Book I. I'm sure this is either RAF's or Garnet's. Vertical photo is 10 x 8. This one is only about 3 x 4. Photo by author.

Fig. 534

Untitled. G.B. Fox. ©. K.T. Co., Cin. Ohio. 7 x 9. Courtesy Dale & Ruth Niemeier.

"Eager for Action." G.B. Fox. 9 1/2 x 7. Courtesy Pat Gibson.

Fig. 535

Fig. 536

Untitled. G.B. Fox. This example is an advertising thermometer. Courtesy Mary & Len Henning.

"A Tense Point." G.B. Fox. Notice the similarity between the front dogs in this and the next print. 8 x 10. Courtesy Pat Gibson.

Fig. 537

Fig. 538

189

"Alert." G.B. Fox. 9 x 7. Courtesy Pat Gibson.

"A Keen Pair." G.B. Fox. 9 x 7.

Fig. 539

Fig. 540

"Poised for Action." (Also titled "A Thoroughbred" -- on a 1947 calendar -- 6 1/2 x 4 1/2.) G.B. Fox. 7 x 5. Found on 1924, 1942, and 1953 calendars. Photo courtesy Pat Gibson.

"Poised for Action" and "Awaiting the Call" on identical calendars (no publisher information). Left to right: 1953, 1924, 1926. Courtesy Ben & Sandra Ross.

Fig. 541

Fig. 541-a

"Awaiting the Call." G. Fawkes. 9 1/2 x 7. Found on 1926 and 1936 calendars. Courtesy Pat Gibson.

Fig. 542

"Set for Action." Publisher's #3813. G.B. Fox. 9 x 7. Courtesy Pat Gibson.

Fig. 543

"King of the Hunt." G.B. Fox. 8 x 6. Courtesy Pat Gibson.

Fig. 544

"The Champion." G.B. Fox. 9 x 7. This print begins what must have been a series by the same publisher. Only one, "The Guardian," carries a publisher's name. Courtesy Nick Morin.

Fig. 545

"The Challenger." G.B. Fox. 9 x 7. Courtesy Pat Gibson.

Fig. 546

"The Aristocrat." G.B. Fox. 9 x 7. Courtesy Pat Gibson.

Fig. 547

"The Diplomat." G.B. Fox. 10 x 7. Courtesy Pat Gibson.

Fig. 548

"The Guardian." G.B. Fox. Morris & Bendien. 9 x 6. Courtesy Pat Gibson.

Fig. 549

"Pal O' Mine." G.B. Fox. 9 x 7. Courtesy Pat Gibson.

"Steamboat Round the Bend." G.B. Fox. 7 x 5, 20 x 16. Courtesy Ben & Sandra Ross.

Fig. 550

Fig. 551

"The Treasure Ship. ©. F.A.S., #7892, Painting by G. Fox. 12 1/4 x 9 1/2. Collection Ann Fox Mergenthaler. Photo by author.

Fig. 552

POSSIBLE PSEUDONYMS AND OTHER CONFUSING SIGNATURES

One of the most exciting features of the "Fox Hunt" has been the artist's use of pseudonyms. Since this information was made public in Book I, several other possibilities have come to light along with one near certainty--Musson. My file of "signed look-alikes" has also grown considerably.

For the benefit of anyone who might not have access to Book One, I will briefly review the pseudonym information introduced there. We know that RAF sometimes used pseudonyms when he wasn't particularly proud of a painting or when a publisher did not want the same artist's name signed to more than one print on a calendar. The names RAF's children agree on are C. Wainright (we find this as Charles or C.N. Wainwright--note the extra "w"), George White, Elmer Lewis and George W. Turner. Bill Fox also believes his father sometimes used the names John Wanright, L. Capelli, John Calvin (most often found as Colvin) and the last name Dupre. The Capelli featured in Book I is the only one I am aware of. Each of these other names, as well as a few additions, is discussed individually in this section.

Charles Stacey is a previously unknown possible pseudonym. According to one of RAF's daughters, Charles Stacey was the husband of Garnet Fox's sister and RAF occasionally used his name. The only print that has been found thus signed is a reverse image of #433, "The Leader."

The signature "Reynard" is still sometimes promoted as a Fox pseudonym. However, we have no evidence to support the theory that Henri G. Reynard is Fox; and "G.T." (Grant Tyson) Reynard most definitely is not.

Also, please remember that the name "A. Fox" was used by Joseph Hoover & Sons to copyright a certain number of their calendar pictures. No "A. Fox" existed, but the company has owned the name since 1908. It may have been used to capitalize on RAF's popularity.

For information on William Thomas, please see the article by Jo Ann Wright in the December 6, 1989, issue of "The Antique Trader."

Finally, notice the information on the name "LeRoy" that accompanies the description of #719. The painting is signed "Leroy" & under the print is written "12 x 36. By the Campfire Glow. Oil, Fox (Leroy)." The People's Art Project (see "Publisher's section) lists three paintings by LeRoy in their files: "Alarm," 1901, a black & white horse; "Puss in Boots," 1904; and "Happy Family" (also cats), 1905. The caption accompanying "Puss in Boots" describes LeRoy as a "famous French cat painter." This is how we discovered "Musson," so LeRoy might be a name to watch.

Having said that, I must emphasize again that a good deal of any discussion on possible pseudonyms is speculation. Neither I, the Fox family, nor the publishers of this book accept any responsibility if any Fox collector purchases a print with one of these signatures and later learns that it was <u>not</u> done by Fox. Also, if any of these names turn out to have belonged to separate artists, they deserve recognition in their own right and we apologize to them and their descendants for any confusion.

For purposes of this book, I have kept the prints of each pseudonym together and have listed in the main text only those pseudonyms that have also been found signed Fox.

The pseudonyms are not priced individually in the accompanying price guide. Most pseudonyms will bring no more than 1/3 to 1/2 the price of a signed RAF. Musson, Elmer Lewis, Wainright and DeForest are the exceptions: Musson and Elmer Lewis are priced almost evenly with signed Fox prints. Wainright and DeForest will bring a little less but still more than the other possible pseudonyms.

A brief discussion of "Other Confusing Signatures" concludes this section.

G. Blanchard Carr

G. Blanchard Carr is a name that came to us from one of RAF's daughters at the 1989 Fox convention in St. Louis. She showed two prints at that time, and several others with this signature have since surfaced.

One enterprising Fox Hunter even pointed out the similarity between "G. Blanchard" and "Garnet Bancroft" (same initials).

Finally, this "Carr" should not be confused with Samuel S. Carr (1837-1908), an American artist who also painted genre, landscape and wildlife scenes. All the Samuel S. Carr (also, S.S. Carr) signatures we've seen are in capital letters. To further the confusion, he also dropped the "tail" of the "A" and each "R" of "CARR" much as RAF did with his "n" and "x." As you will see in the detail of "A Haven of Splendor," the G. Blanchard Carr" signature is quite different.

"The Garden Home." G. Blanchard Carr. Morris & Bendien Inc., N.Y. 12 x 9, 14 x 10. Jaegers collection. Photo by author.

"Watching." B. Carr. The house and additional sheep at left midground may not be visible in this photo. 5 x 7. Courtesy Pat Gibson.

Fig. 553

Fig. 554

"The Grandeur of Summer." G.B. Carr. Publisher's #8302. ©. Great Britain. Printed in U.S.A. Published by St. Lawrence Frame & Glass Co., Montreal. (At the center, lower edge [in the grass] is handwritten, ©. M. & B., N.Y.) Courtesy Richard & Laura Goldfarb.

"A Haven of Splendor." G. Blanchard Carr. Publisher's #8301. Morris & Bendien Co., N.Y. 10 x14. Collection Ann Fox Mergenthaler. Photo by author.

Fig. 555

Fig. 556

Detail from Fig. 556 shows signature.

Fig. 556-a

"Cozy Cottage." G. Blanchard Carr. Publisher's #8503. Morris & Bendien Co. 14 x 10.
Collection Ann Fox Mergenthaler. Photo by author.

Fig. 557

John Calvin/Colvin

John Calvin was among the names suggested as possible pseudonyms by RAF's son who suspected a connection between the name of the early American Puritan and the fact that RAF's father was a Methodist minister. However, the name often appears as "John Colvin" or "J. Colvin." This could be an artifact of the printing process or a mistake by the publisher--it can be difficult to distinguish between an "a" and an "o"-- or it could indicate to us that someone named John Colvin existed and painted without any connection whatever to R. Atkinson Fox. Still, Fig. 402, which we have now found signed "Colvin," was owned by RAF's son and believed by him to have been painted by his father. Since then, a number of "Colvins" have been found that mimic the work of Fox.

"A Faithful Guardian." 9 x 12. Courtesy Duane & Dolores Ramsey

"Chums." J. Colvin. 20 x 16. Courtesy Pat Gibson.

Fig. 558

Fig. 559

Untitled. J. Colvin. 14 1/2 x 10 3/4. Courtesy Duane & Dolores Ramsey.

"On Guard." J. Colvin. Publisher's #5363. Found on a 1920 calendar. 6 x 4 1/4. Courtesy Duane & Dolores Ramsey.

Fig. 560

Fig. 561

This larger version of "On Guard" shows more of the little girl but cuts off the pull toy in front. 13 x 16. Courtesy Pat Gibson. In both prints, the bow in the little girls hair and the one around the kitten-toy's neck are bright red.

Fig. 561-a

"Playmates." J. Colvin. Found on a 1922 calendar. 11 x 16. Courtesy Rink Thornton.

Fig. 562

"Faithful." J. Colvin. Both these little girls are dressed in blue.

Fig. 563

"Disputed Property." J. Colvin. Found with publisher's #'s 3526 & 3617. © 1912 E.C. Cutler & A.M. Collins Mfg. Co. 1914 salesman's sample calendar. Image is 7 x 11. Courtesy Ben & Sandra Ross.

Fig. 564

201

"Their First Lesson." J. Colvin. Found on a 1916 calendar. 10 x 11. Courtesy Pat Gibson.

Fig. 565

"Their Great Day." John Colvin. Publisher's #590. Compare this to Fig. 216 [#144]. Found on a fan by Pat Gibson.

Fig. 566

In this print, the artist's name is handprinted, "John Colvin," instead of the script, "J. Colvin" of most prints. Here, it is apparent that the "Tail" of the "h" and each "n" is carried below the line, like the "k" and each "n" in RAF's signature.

Fig. 566-a

"Close Friends." J. Colvin. 10 x 8. Courtesy Duane & Dolores Ramsey.

Fig. 567

202

Untitled. J. Colvin. Found on a tablet cover by Margene Petros.

Untitled. J. Colvin. The gruesome details of this print may be difficult to make out in b&w, so I will describe it. Four men are around a campfire. One man (in buckskins, with a rifle across his lap) points off to his left where a deer hangs by one leg from a tree. 7 1/2 x 9. Courtesy Hugh Hetzer.

Fig. 568

Fig. 569

Arthur DeForest

Arthur DeForest is one of the names suggested by RAF's son as a pseudonym. It was one I felt least comfortable with, and I could argue either side. I didn't like the photographic quality of some of the portraits. However, RAF started his career as a portrait painter. And we know that some prints of this time period--not necessarily RAF's--<u>did</u> start as photographs.

Some of the prints of children, for example, look like the subject is superimposed upon a prepared background of "A Perfect Melody," for example, but I have a problem believing that he would have elongated the figure of the woman in such a manner.

Finally, we were all ready to accept "The Silence Unbroken" as DeForest/Fox until we learned that it was by George DeForest <u>Brush</u>. (<u>Then</u> one turned up signed "Wainwright"!)

Well, as I said, these doubts plagued our minds until Chris McCann, who is researching a book on puzzles, found a puzzle of "The Adventuress." I had this print on file as DeForest. Chris's puzzle is also signed DeForest, but a publisher's print of the image inside the puzzle box is signed R.A. Fox. There are minute differences in the two images, but you have to have them side-by-side and look hard to see them.

Does this <u>prove</u> that DeForest was Fox? Not really. But added to the existing evidence, it adds up to a strong argument in favor of the pseudonym. Besides, the work signed DeForest is of such quality and desirability that I don't think anyone would be too disappointed with their DeForest prints even if they turned out to not be Fox.

This print was reported by three different Fox Hunters as untitled and signed "George DeForest Brush." Sizes are 9 x 7, 12 1/2 x 9 1/4 and 16 1/2 x 13. Courtesy Barb Kratz. It has also been found titled "Quiet Solitude" and attributed, "Painting by Wainwright," 8 x 14. The same image, with a slightly different background was found on a page of "The Mentor," Vol. 3, No. 9, Serial No. 85, 1915. It is titled, "The Silence Broken." (Brush, by the way, is also listed in American Artists at Auction as a painter who lived from 1855-1941 and specialized in painting figures.)

"The Adventuress." DeForest. 9 1/2 x 7, 13 1/2 x 11. Also found on the lid of a candy box. Courtesy Pat Gibson

Fig. 572

No. 18, "The Adventuress," found as a publisher's insert in a puzzle. The puzzle itself is signed R.A. Fox. Note slight differences in the hat and cuff of left boot. Thanks to Chris McCann.

No. 18. The Adventuress

PUZZLE SIGNED
"DE FOREST"
PICTURE SLIGHTLY DIFFERENT

Fig. 570

Fig. 572-a

"On Treasure Isle." DeForest. 9 x 7. Courtesy Pat Gibson.

Fig. 573

"The Children's Hour." DeForest. Print is 8 x 6, found on a 1926 calendar by Pat Gibson.

Fig. 574

"A Perfect Melody." DeForest. 9 1/2 x 7. Courtesy Pat Gibson.

Fig. 575

"Esmeralda." DeForest. This is my favorite and, in my opinion, the most Fox-like of the DeForest portraits. 9 x 7. Courtesy Margene Petros.

Fig. 576

"Mother's Darling." DeForest. 8 x 6. Courtesy Pat Gibson

Fig. 577

"Mighty Like a Rose." DeForest. 8 x 6. Richard & Laura Goldfarb. Check out the baby in "Mother's Darling." This could be the same child a year or so later.

Fig. 578

"A Bounty from Heaven." DeForest. 7 7/8 x 5 7/8 calendar print. Courtesy Ben & Sandra Ross.

Fig. 579

"Age of Innocence." DeForest. This little girl is holding a doll in her lap. 7 x 5. Courtesy Pat Gibson.

Fig. 580

"He Loves Me, He Loves Me Not." DeForest. 8 x 6. Courtesy Duane & Dolores Ramsey.

Fig. 581

"Childhood Days." DeForest. 10 x 8. Courtesy Pat Gibson. I think this is a little boy sitting on the ground, and I think he's the same boy that appears in "Playmates" and "A Barrel of Fun."

Fig. 582

"Playmates." DeForest. 10 x 8. Courtesy Duane & Dolores Ramsey

Fig. 583

"Teasing." DeForest. Gerlach-Barklow. 8 x 10. Courtesy Margene & Terry Petros.

Fig. 584

"Honest and Truly." DeForest. Gerlach-Barklow. 8 x 10. Courtesy Margene & Terry Petros.

Fig. 585

"A Barrel of Fun." DeForest. 10 x 8. Found on a 1929 calendar by Duane & Dolores Ramsey.

Fig. 586

"Speak Rover." DeForest. 9 x 7. Courtesy Pat Gibson

Fig. 587

"Strictly Confidential." DeForest. 10 x 8. Courtesy Duane & Dolores Ramsey.

Fig. 588

Dupre

Dupre is another of the names suggested as possible pseudonyms by RAF's children. We really don't know much about the name--we don't even have a first name to go with it. However, this Dupre should not be confused with Julian Dupre (1851-1910), the French painter whose "The Ballon" hangs in the Metropolitan Museum of Art (someday, RAF!). Julien Dupre painted landscapes and animals, but a listing of his paintings sold at auction does not include any of the titles we have listed as Dupre.

Grasping at straws, some of us have noticed that the "D" in DeForest and the "D" in Dupre are similar. Others have pointed out that Dupre's "Wanetah" and "The Chieftain's Pride," and Deforest's "Pride of the Blue Ridge" (see Book I) could have been painted from the same model.

"Wanetah." Dupre. 10 x 8. Courtesy Wm. C. & Becky Fox.

Fig. 589

"The Chieftain's Pride." Dupre. This, along with four other prints (one Wainright & one RAF), has been found in identical salesman's sample folders-- one titled "The new Rembrandt Art Calendar Offering" and the other titled "The new Stratford Art Calendar Offering." The latter was published by John Baumgarth Co., Chicago. 16 1/2 x 9. Courtesy Wm. C. & Becky Fox.

Fig. 590

"The Land of Sky Blue Waters." Dupre. 10 x 8, 16 x 10. Courtesy Deanna Hulse.

Fig. 591

The exact Indian girl from Dupre's "The Land of Sky Blue Waters" has been found--reversed--in an unsigned night scene titled "Ramona." Courtesy Laura Hayward.

Fig. 591-a

"Aloya of the South Seas." Dupre. 9 1/2 x 7. Courtesy Duane & Dolores Ramsey.

Fig. 592

"The Grandeur of Nature." Dupre. 8 x 6, 10 x 8. Courtesy Pat Gibson.

Fig. 594

"By the Zuider Zee." Dupre. According to my encyclopedia, the Zuider Zee was an arm of the North Sea. In 1932, it was closed by a 20-mile dike between Holland and Friesland. This changed the Zuider Zee into a fresh-water lake known as IJsselmeer. By the way, the figure of a person is visible in the doorway of the windmill. 7 x 9 1/2. Found in a salesman's sample "Stratford" portfolio published by "John Baumgarth Publishing Co., Chicago, Il." by Nick Morin.

Fig. 593

"Dreamy Valley." Dupre. A farmhouse, outbuildings and more cows are visible in the far right background. Autumn colors. 10 x 8. Courtesy Ben & Sandra Ross.

"At Peace With the World." Dupre. This is a faint, twilight scene; I'm sure the details will be difficult to make out, so I'll describe it. Two men are herding a flock of sheep toward the viewer. A very small creek or pond (or a large puddle) is at left foreground. Behind the sheep is a red wagon and, at right, two horses stand in the doorway of a barn that has smoke coming out of its chimney. Part of a house is just visible at far left midground. Trees, pink clouds in background. 9 1/2 x 7. Courtesy Duane & Dolores Ramsey.

Fig. 595

Fig. 596

Elmer Lewis
"H." Lewis

Elmer Lewis is one of the few pseudonyms that we feel pretty secure about. As one of the ladies who presented the "People's Art Project" findings to the 1989 Fox convention remarked, "There just can be no doubt that Elmer Lewis is Fox." More often than not, if you find an Elmer Lewis, you've found a big cat. However, we also have some other animals, a few landscapes, and even a couple of military prints all signed Elmer Lewis.

Of H. Lewis, we are not nearly so certain. RAF's son first suggested that RAF may have used "Henry Lewis"--Henry being the name of the artist's father. "Henry," then, might have been shortened to "H" and so we have "H. Lewis." Another possibility is that in the process of lending and borrowing, and buying and selling among publishers, the "E" of Elmer Lewis might somewhere have been mistaken for an "H" and the mistake was then perpetuated. "Elmer Lewis" is usually found in a neat cursive--probably the same hand that penned "R.A. Fox" for the Thos. D. Murphy Co. The "H. Lewis" signature is different. At any rate, we have far more prints signed Elmer Lewis than are signed H. Lewis, and H. Lewis remains a signature to approach with extreme caution.

Untitled. Elmer Lewis. This is Fig. 399 from Book I. I wanted you to see it as this 6 x 4 1/2 calendar top with the inscription, "Half the battle is in being on the hilltop first, the other half in staying there." Courtesy Barb Kratz.

Fig. 597

"Strength and Security." Painting by Elmer Lewis. ©. 1916, Elwood Myers Co., Springfield, Ohio. As you will see, we have a "Strength" and a "Security" by Elmer Lewis. And this old fellow exemplifies both. Isn't he wonderful? 15 x 22. Courtesy Pat Gibson.

Fig. 598

"Security." Elmer Lewis. Publisher's #9662. 9 1/2 x 12, 16 x 20. Courtesy Duane & Dolores Ramsey.

Fig. 599

"Safely Guarded." Elmer Lewis. This is on the People's Art Project (PAP) list for 1926 and 1933. It has been found on a 1927 calendar. Barely visible, at top right, is an eagle that the lioness is "guarding" her cubs from. 16 x 20. Courtesy Margene & Terry Petros.

Fig. 600

"The Guardian." Elmer Lewis. PAP list for 1925 & 1927. 16 x 22. Courtesy Duane & Dolores Ramsey.

"Safe and Secure." Elmer Lewis. 9 x 12, 16 x 20. Courtesy Duane & Dolores Ramsey.

Fig. 601

Fig. 602

"Master of All He Surveys." Elmer Lewis. 8 x 10. Courtesy Pat Gibson.

"Monarch of All He Surveys." Elmer Lewis. 7 1/2 x 5 1/2. Courtesy Duane & Dolores Ramsey.

Fig. 603

Fig. 604

"A Royal Pair." Elmer Lewis. On PAP list for 1928. 21 3/4 x 16 3/4. Courtesy Bill Richardson.

"Old Ocean Roars, the Jungle Answers." Elmer Lewis. PAP list for 1928. This has also been found titled "Defiance;" and it has been found as a "Weekly Picture Puzzle," titled "Lions at Sunset." 8 1/4 x 11 1/4. Collection Ann Fox Mergenthaler. Photo by author.

Fig. 605

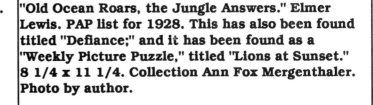

Fig. 606

Untitled. Elmer Lewis. 7 x 9, 10 x 13 1/2. Collection Ann Fox Mergenthaler. Photo by author.

"Ever Watchful." Elmer Lewis. Publishers #8221. 9 1/2 x 11. Courtesy Duane & Dolores Ramsey.

Fig. 607

Fig. 608

"Discretion is the Better Part of Valor." Elmer Lewis. This is on the PAP list for 1918 & 1930, and has also been found on a 1918 calendar. (Compare this to #442, [Fig. 444], "The Monarchs.") 6 x 9. Courtesy Pat Gibson

"Untamed Monarchs." Elmer Lewis. (This is both signed--although the signature is printed this time--and marked "Painting by Elmer Lewis.") ©. 1912, Ketterling Litho. Mfg. Co. 8 3/4 x 10 3/4. Found on a 1913 calendar by Ben & Sandra Ross.

Fig. 609

Fig. 610

"On the Lookout." Elmer Lewis. Printed on the back: "Print #)D-1729, ©. TDM Co., Red Oak, Ia. This is on the PAP list for 1917. You almost have to have this print and "On A Trail" side-by-side to differentiate between the tigers. 10 1/4 x 16. Collection Ann Fox Mergenthaler. Photo by author.

"On A Trail." Elmer Lewis. Publisher's #2732. The ledge and background of this painting differ from "On the Lookout." Here, the tigers are looking at a caravan of men and camels crossing the valley below. But the two pairs of tigers remind me of those "Can You Find the Differences?" children's puzzles. Only the mouths and tails of the tigers are slightly different. 7 x 9. Courtesy Ben & Sandra Ross.

Fig. 611

Fig. 612

"A Critical Moment." Elmer Lewis. This tiger is trying to sneak up on a deer visible in the background. 6 x 8. Courtesy Pat Gibson.

"Strength." Elmer Lewis. Publisher's #4016. ©. F.A.S. This leopard has spotted a deer or elk far in the right background. This print has been found on a 1913 sample calendar. 10 x 13. The example shown is from Ann Fox Mergenthaler's collection. Photo by author.

Fig. 613

Fig. 614

"On Rocky Heights." Elmer Lewis. Marked, "H.C. Tack 12, ©. 1913, Brown & Bigelow, St. Paul, USA." 9 x 4 3/4. Courtesy Ben & Sandra Ross.

"A Battle Royal." Elmer Lewis. 8 x 12. Collection Ann Fox Mergenthaler. Photo by author.

Fig. 615

Fig. 616

"Washington at Headquarters." Elmer Lewis. Publisher's #8227. 6 x 8, 10 x 11. Courtesy at Bobye & Chris Syverson.

"Washington at the Battle of Monmouth." Elmer Lewis. Publisher's #1408. 8 x 6, 12 x 9, 19 x 16. Found on a 1919 calendar by Pat Gibson.

Fig. 617

Fig. 618

"The Grip of Winter." Elmer Lewis. 10 x 3. Courtesy Duane & Dolores Ramsey.

Untitled. Elmer Lewis. This is a dark night scene with trees framing a small inlet marked by a fallen log under a cloudy sky. 10 x 13 1/2. Courtesy Pat Gibson.

Fig. 619

Fig. 620

"The Lure of the Lake." Elmer Lewis. ©. 1924 by American Art Works, Coshocton, Ohio. In terms of the trees, water, sky--and even the fallen log, this print is very similar to the previous one. That dot on the water in the background is a canoe with two more figures in it. 10 x 13 1/2. Courtesy Pat Gibson

Untitled. H. Lewis. Keystone Picture Frame Co., Pgh., Pa., USA. Dec., 1926. Courtesy Wm. C. & Becky Fox.

Fig. 621

Fig. 622

Untitled. H. Lewis. 14 x 22. Courtesy Pat Gibson.

Untitled. H. Lewis. Keystone Picture Co., Pittsburgh. 14 x 22. Courtesy Lee Fenner.

Fig. 623

Fig. 624

221

"Asters." H. Lewis. Keystone Picture Frame Co., Pittsburgh, Pa. 16 x 20. Courtesy Barb Kratz.

Untitled. H. Lewis. Keystone Picture Frame Co., Pgh. Pa. This looks like it might be a portion of another, more complete print. 22 x 14. Courtesy Mark & Carol Graham.

Fig. 625

Fig. 626

Musson

We first became aware of the name "Musson" from one of the painting records of Thomas D. Murphy Co. At the lower left of page 43, Book I, "After the Harvest" is listed as having been painted by R.Atkinson Fox, and "H. Musson" is written above RAF. I drew attention to this discussing the pseudonyms on page 133 of that book.

Since that time, we have found a number of Mussons; several of them can be identified on the Painting Records of the Thos. D. Murphy Co. shown on pp 42-44 of Book I--all of these show RAF as the artist. We find the name as "Musson," "H. Musson," "Ed. Musson" and "Edw. Musson." Finally, the organizers of the People's Art Project, as well as a woman who worked for Thos. D. Murphy Co. for a number of years, have concurred that there can be little doubt, if any, that Musson is Fox.

"In the Pasture." (Fox list #430) Publisher's #4550. Also titled, "A Proud Mother." Publisher's #4326. Signed R.A. Fox, and attributed to H. Musson in a 1903 Thos D. Murphy Co. catalog. (Also see Painting Record #77, pg. 43, Book I). This is one of the few pseudonyms on the Fox list (see Fig. 392). That's because it was found with the sig. R. Atkinson Fox and listed before it was found with the Musson reference. Sizes listed on the painting record are 8 x 6 1/2 and 10 1/4 x 8 1/4. Each size has a different series number and was produced by a different company. Photo by author from a 1903 Thos. D. Murphy Co. catalog owned by Margene & Terry Petros.

"When the Cows Come Home." H. Musson. Publisher's #4234. ©. 1901, Thos. D. Murphy Co., Red Oak, Ia. See Painting Record #88, bottom right, page 43, Book I. Series #4234 was reproduced in 8 x 6 1/2, by the Electro-Tint Co. in 1902. Courtesy Sharon Gergen.

Fig. 628

Untitled. H. Musson 3 1/2 x 5 1/2. Courtesy Pat Gibson.

Fig. 627

Fig. 629

"Evening." (Fox list #691) Publisher's #4319. Signed R.A. Fox. Attributed to H. Musson. ©. 1902, TDM Co. Described on Painting Record #74, pg. 43, Book I. Cows coming down lane. Farmhouse to left. Trees to right. Photographed from TDM Co. catalog. Courtesy Barb Kratz.

In this close-up, you can clearly see that the painting is signed R.A. Fox. Photo by author.

Fig. 631

Fig. 631-a

"At Eventide." H. Musson. Thos. D. Murphy Co. Courtesy People's Art Project, and JII/Sales Promotion Associates, Red Oak, Iowa.

"The Farm Yard." Musson. Publisher's #647. ©. 1903, The Thos. D. Murphy Co., Red Oak, Ia. Photographed from a 1903 TDM Co. catalog. Also see Painting Record #20, pg. 42, Book I. Courtesy Margene & Terry Petros.

Fig. 632

Fig. 633

"Making a Dicker." H. Musson. Thos. D. Murphy Co. Courtesy People's Art Project, and JII/Sales Promotion Associates, Red Oak, Iowa.

Fig. 636

"Homeward Bound." (Fox list #692) Publisher's #4316. Sgnd. R.A. Fox. Attributed to H. Musson. ©. 1902, TDM Co. Check Painting Record #515, pg. 44, Book I. Appears on the People's Art Project list for 1903. Photographed from a TDM Co. catalog. Courtesy Barb Kratz.

Fig. 637

"Under the Maples." H. Musson. Publisher's #614. ©. 1906, Thos. D. Murphy Co. Courtesy Pat Gibson.

Fig. 638

"After the Harvest." (Fox list #690) Publisher's #4314. No signature. Attributed to H. Musson. ©. 1902, TDM Co. See Painting Record, bottom left corner, pg. 43, Book I: "Wheat Field in shocks. Chickens in foreground. Blue sky." This painting record was the first indication we had of Musson as a pseudonym. Photographed from TDM Co. catalog. Courtesy Barb Kratz.

Fig. 639

"A Bold Protector." Edw. Musson. Thos. D. Murphy Co. Courtesy People's Art Project, and JII/Sales Promotion Associates, Red Oak, Iowa.

"Waiting for Orders." Edw. Musson. Thos. D. Murphy Co. Courtesy People's Art Project, and JII/Sales Promotion Associates, Red Oak, Iowa.

Fig. 640

Fig. 641

"A Thoroughbred." Edw. Musson. Publisher's #635. See Painting Record #81, pg. 42, Book I. Series 6355 was reproduced in 4 3/4 x 6 3/4, by the Electro-Tint Engraving Co. in 1903.
Photo by author from a 1903 Thos. D. Murphy Co. catalog owned by Margene & Terry Petros.

Fig. 642

"Four of a Kind." Musson. Publisher's #4337. Photo by author from a
1903 Thos. D. Murphy Co. catalog owned by Margene & Terry Petros.

Fig. 643

"An Interesting Family." Edw. Musson. Publisher's #2217. See Painting Record #85, pg. 43, Book I.
Series 2217 was reproduced in 7 x 10 1/2, by the Electro-Tint Co. in 1902. Unfortunately, this paint-
ing was included on a record of "Paintings Destroyed per Mr. Cochrane and T.D. Murphy, July 8, 1940."
It was listed as #92, "An Interesting Family--Fox." Courtesy Barb Kratz

Fig. 644

228

George W. Turner

Only two prints signed George W. Turner have surfaced since Book I, bringing our number of Turner prints to a grand total of three! ("Silvery Grandeur, Fig. 418, Book I, was presumed to be Turner because it is so similar to "The Silvery Divide" (Fig. 417, Book I) and because it was signed "Geo. W" as if the rest of the signature had been cut. It has since been found with a complete signature--"Geo. White.") "The Silvery Divide" is still the one that shows up most frequently.

"Off New England Shores." Geo. W. Turner. 10 x 8. Courtesy Duane & Dolores Ramsey.

"Neath Sunset Skies." Geo W. Turner. 10 1/4 x 8. Courtesy Duane & Dolores Ramsey.

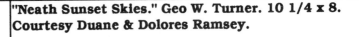

Fig. 645

Fig. 646

Charles (C.N.) Wain(w)right

In my very homemade Pseudonym Guide, put together in 1988 as a way of distributing pseudonym information, I introduced Wainright as "almost certainly a pseudonym." As an English teacher, I can appreciate that oxymoron. Cautious optimism. The signature sometimes reads Charles (or Chs.), sometimes C.N. and sometimes just C. Wain(w)right. We even have a Thos. Wainright, an F. Wainright, and one C. Wain.

The last name most often eliminates the middle "w." Several possible reasons have been suggested. One is simply that if RAF made this name up, he himself might have sometimes forgotten exactly how he intended to spell it. Another possibility is that whoever signed a particular print at the publisher or printer might have varied the spelling. I can't always be certain I am reporting the spelling correctly for a particular print. I have had letters in which someone reports that a print is signed "Wainright" when I can clearly see the signature on the photo is "Wainwright" and vice-versa. I can't always see the signature, so sometimes I have to rely on what is reported to me.

Finally, I don't want to reprint pictures that appeared in Book I, but I would like for you to know that at one time, Fig. 405, "Paradise" by Wainright, was offered on stationery by the "Art Guild" in Minneapolis.

"A View Through the Timber." Chs. Wainright. 9 x 6. Courtesy Duane & Dolores Ramsey.

"Under the Greenwood Tree." Chs. Wainright. 6 x 9, 9 1/2 x 12. Courtesy Duane & Dolores Ramsey.

Fig. 647

Fig. 648

"The Flavor of Fall." Chs. Wainright. Shows a publisher's #622 at bottom right. 9 1/2 x 12. (Have you ever seen a Fox Hunter remove his or her glasses and peer closely at a print? It's because we're all nearsighted from trying to distinguish between prints like this and "Under the Greenwood Tree.") Courtesy Duane & Dolores Ramsey.

"The Old Pathway." Publisher's #1110. Painting by Chs. Wainwright. ©. F.A. Schneider. 8 x 13, 9 1/2 x 6 1/2.

Fig. 649

Fig. 650

"The Old Pathway." A different perspective was achieved when the publisher focused on one aspect of the painting and enclosed it in an oval.

Fig. 650-a

"Overlooking Emerald Bay." C.N. Wainwright. 10 x 8. Courtesy Duane & Dolores Ramsey.

Fig. 651

"At Sundown in the Golden West." C. Wainwright. In a lovely, art-deco calendar mount. 9 1/2 x 7. Courtesy Duane & Dolores Ramsey.

Fig. 652

"The Campers." Wainright. 12 x 6. Compare to Elmer Lewis, "The Lure of the Lake." Courtesy Ben & Sandra Ross.

Fig. 653

"The Echoing Call." C. Wainright. 10 x 8. Courtesy Duane & Dolores Ramsey

Fig. 654

"Fra Longfellow Glen." We know that a German magazine, "Die Hausfrau," published some works by Garnet (G.B. Fox). Now comes this print with the words "Fra Longfellow Glen, efter original maleri av Chr Wainright." This means either: 1) This is a print titled "Longfellow Glen" made from a painting by Charles Wainright, or 2) Someone named Glen Longfellow copied this painting from Wainright. 11 3/4 x 8. Courtesy Barb Kratz.

Fig. 655

Untitled. C.N. Wainwright. This print has also been found apparently signed "M-Lowell" with a printed copyright symbol directly above it. Other prints (not Fox) have been reported with this mark, as if Lowell were the artist. With the dash in the "signature" and the proximity to copyright symbols and numbers, I would be inclined to think "M-Lowell" is some kind of publisher or printer rather than an artist. However, to further confuse the issue, there is a Milton Lowell (1848-1927) who specialized in landscapes listed in American Artists at Auction, 1645-1945. 7 x 11. Courtesy Pat Gibson.

Fig. 656

"Paradise Valley." C.N. Wainright. 10 x 8. Courtesy Pat Gibson.

Fig. 657

"A Garden of Flowers." C. Wainwright. Sample calendar print. 17 x 9 1/2. Courtesy Nick Morin.

"A Garden of Flowers" on an advertising fan. Courtesy Wm. C. & Becky Fox.

Fig. 658

Fig. 658-a

"The House by the Side of the Road." C. Wainright. This, along with four other prints (one Dupre & one RAF), has been found in identical salesman's sample folders--one titled "The new Rembrandt Art Calendar Offering." The latter was published by John Baumgarth Co., Chicago. Overall size of the calendar was 16 1/2 x 9. Also found in 7 x 9 1/2. Courtesy Nick Morin.

"100% Pure." Chs. Wainwright. Also reported with title, "Down on the Farm." 8 1/2 x 10 1/2. Courtesy Pat Gibson.

Fig. 659

Fig. 660

"The Old Fishing Hole." C.N. Wainwright. 10 x 8. Courtesy Duane & Dolores Ramsey. Compare this little fisherboy to the one in #384 (Fig. 282), "Down by the Bridge." 10 x 8. Courtesy Duane & Dolores Ramsey.

Fig. 661

"Me and Dixie." Thos. Wainright. 7 x 9. Courtesy Duane & Dolores Ramsey.

Fig. 662

"The Favorite." C. Wain. This signature is at the bottom left, so it can't be the result of a trimmed print. However, it is written in tiny, neat letters, just like so many of the Wain(w)right pictures are signed--and it looks right. 7 x 5. Courtesy Pat Gibson.

Fig. 663

"Maid in USA." C. Wainright. Print is 8 x 6. Found on a 1922 advertising calendar by Wm. C. & Becky Fox.

Fig. 664

"Being Helpful." F. Wainright. 8 x 6. Found on a 1929 calendar by Pat Gibson.

Fig. 665

"The Unbroken Bond of Friendship." Chs. Wainright. The American Art Works Inc., Coshocton, Ohio. Other than the suggestion by RAF's children that Wain(w)right was a possible pseudonym, the first solid evidence we had in this direction was when Melvin & Lois Trimble found Fig. 29 is an oil painting titled "George Washington Greeting LaFayette at Valley Forge," and signed R. Atkinson Fox. The Trimbles' print is 9 x 7.

Fig. 666

"Washington and LaFayette at Valley Forge." Chs. Wainright. The American Art Works Inc., Coshocton, Ohio. Pat Gibson found the same image on an advertising fan.

Fig. 666-a

"Quiet Solitude." Painting by Wainwright. This has also been found signed "DeForest" and "George DeForest Brush," with a short biography of that artist. 8 x 14. Courtesy Nick Morin.

Fig. 667

George White

George White is another of the possible pseudonyms about which we know next to nothing. It was one of the names suggested by RAF's sons who first introduced me to the possible pseudonyms. This signature, too, varies from print to print.

"At the Foot of Mount Rainier." G.L. White. John Baumgarth Co., Chicago. Calendar top. 8 x 6, 10 x 8. Courtesy Wm. C. & Becky Fox.

"Monarch of the Wilderness." Chs. L. Wilson. Compare the elk in this print to the elk in White's "At the Foot of Mount Rainier," The backgrounds are different. 10 x 8. Courtesy Wm. C. & Becky Fox.

Fig. 668

Fig. 668-a

"Silvery Wonderland." Geo. W. White. 10 x 8. Courtesy Pat Gibson.

Fig. 669

"Silvery Grandeur." This is Fig. 418 in Book I. We thought it was by Geo. W. Turner because it is so similar to his Fig. 417 and was found signed "Geo. W" ... we figured the rest of the signature had been cut off. Well, it had been, but when one was found with a complete signature, the signature was Geo. White. This print was even found on a wastebasket! 9 x 6 3/4, 10 x 8. Courtesy Donna Robinson.

Fig. 670

"The Girl of the Golden West." Geo. White. That's the face of a woman the cowboy is imagining in the clouds at upper left. 8 x 6. Courtesy Pat Gibson.

Fig. 671

"The Sentinel of the Night." G. White. Publisher's #2504. 19 1/2 x 16, 8 x 6. Courtesy Duane & Dolores Ramsey

Fig. 672

"On the Trail." Geo. White. 8 x 8. Courtesy Pat Gibson.

"Scenting the Trail." Geo. W. White. 10 x 8. Courtesy Pat Gibson.

Fig. 673

"All Set." Geo. W. White. Unsigned versions of this print have been found titled "On the Scent." Calendar print. It was apparently published, along with other dog prints, as part of a series titled "Hunter's Friends." 8 x 6. Courtesy Ben & Sandra Ross.

Fig. 675

Fig. 674

George Wood

We have only one print signed George Wood. The name was introduced at the 1989 Fox convention by a woman who worked for Thos. D. Murphy Co. for a number of years. She showed a Painting Record (#2141) that shows the artist as George Wood with "R.A. Fox" written above the artist's name. There is no title, but the painting is described as "Big St. Bernard lying down with little girl asleep on him. Ball on floor-- red plush drapes behind them." No printings are recorded. A later sales record shows painting #2141, "Safely Guarded," artist--Wood, was sold.

Of course, we have the Elmer Lewis "Safely Guarded" and #340 (dog & sheep) titled "Safely Guarded." (Did someone say this gets confusing?) And compare the above description to "On Guard" signed Colvin.

Finally, the one "Geo. Wood" we have on file is similar to other RAF paintings and pseudonyms.

"By a Falling Crystal Stream." George Wood. Print owned by Duane & Dolores Ramsey. Photo by author.

"By a Falling Crystal Stream," unsigned, on an advertising fan. Courtesy Wm. C. & Becky Fox.

Fig. 676

Fig. 676-a

... And Other Confusing Signatures

Among the myriad files that have grown from this project is one labeled "Signed Look-alikes." Arranged by artist's name, it contains photos of prints that, for one reason or another, someone thinks it might be RAF painting under still another name.

Some confusing signatures don't even suggest another artist--they are just confusing. For example, in Book One, I explained that for a time in Chicago, RAF shared studio space with the photographer, Beatrice Tonneson. Recently, several early 1920's Dow Co. prints have surfaced that resemble RAF's portrait work and are marked simply, "Tonneson Studio." This raises several questions: Did Tonneson paint, too? Did RAF instruct her? Did he paint from her photographs? Did she photograph his paintings? Will we ever know?

Some prints actually seem to have been painted by two artists. An untitled "housescape" in the Wainwright section sometimes carries the additional 'signature,' "M-Lowell." At least one other print in "signed Look-alikes" also carries two apparent signatures.

Perhaps the best-known example is Fig. 238, Book One, which is sometimes credited "Fox--Urgelles." Recently, other prints have surfaced marked simply, "Urgelles." Is Fig. 238, then, the result of a collaboration between two artists? We know that publishers were pretty independent when it came to reproducing the work of artists whose work they had purchased. They used various names on an artist's work, for example, and portioned scenes out to the point of getting as many as seven different "sizes" out of one print. We have even learned of cases where a publisher cut a scene out of one canvas and glued it on the background of another, creating a brand-new scene. Perhaps an attack of conscience required putting both artists' names on the resulting print

"Indian at Prayer." W. Gordon Fox. 10 1/2 x 11. Courtesy Pat Gibson.

"The Scout." W. Gordon Fox. ©. 1914, T.M. Stone. 8 x 6. Courtesy Pat Gibson.

Fig. 677

"Next to Nature's Heart." Also found titled, "Anxious Moments." Gordon H. Fox. 11 x 8. Courtesy Pat Gibson.

Fig. 679

Fig. 678

242

"A Day in the Open." J.A. Atkins. Black-and-white, 1932 calendar print. 11 x 8. Courtesy Pat Gibson.

Untitled. F.A. Robert. Compare this to Fig. 261, Book One. 9 x 7. Courtesy Pat Gibson.

Fig. 680

Fig. 681

Other prints are intriguing because in addition to resembling RAF's work, the signature suggests a play on RAF's name. The signature "F.A. Robert," for example. This is like "Robert A. Fox" backward. And the untitled picture is very similar to a know Fox print.

The name "Gordon W. Fox" appears on a couple of Native American scenes and one picturing an elk in snow. The Indians seem very different from RAF's style, but the deer, the snow-covered trees, the mountain in background could easily be RAF.

"A Day in the Open," signed J.A. Atkins, is so much like RAF's work that every time I look at it, go back through "Beautiful Young Women With Horses" just to make sure I haven't missed it somehow.

Finally, there is the issue of the "Prudential" kids. These prints of babies and children that appeared on the covers of "Prudential" magazine in the 1930's are signed, simply, "Fox." Without actually seeing the signature, and with reservations about style, I let myself be persuaded to list the first few. Others came fast and furious.

For two years, I "corresponded" with the Prudential Company. I was referred to one person at one address, then another. Every once in awhile, someone would offer just enough encouragement to keep me searching; but for the most part, my letters went unanswered and my telephone calls were not returned. Finally, I was told that Prudential's back issues are "hermetically sealed" and are opened only occasionally "for major institutions with large grants."

With no way to verify who actually painted these children and signed the pictures "Fox," and with the Fox family giving "thumbs down" to the question, I have sadly removed the Prudential kids from the Fox list. It isn't easy for a mother to disown small children.

It is my fond hope that somewhere, soon, a stack of "Prudential" back issues will surface and buried inside one of them will be an article on the "Fox" who painted the Prudential kids.

Here are some other confusing signatures on "Signed Look-alikes" that I would like to know more about:

Charles Alexander	Ashton Day	Edward Eggleston
H. Faben	Arthur Garratt	Roy Gross
George Hacker	Steve Hacker	Henri G. Reynard
George Hood	Chs. Morgan	Byron G. Newton
Hermann Rudisuhli	Urgelles	C.K. Van Nortwick
E. West	R. Whitman	H. Whitroy
Chs. Wilson*	R. Wilson*	

*There are a Charles (Theller) Wilson and a Robert (Burns) Wilson listed in American Artists at Auction. However, these are common names, and the descriptions of their work and time don't quite fit.

"Buddies." Sgnd. Fox (Like #319). Cover for "Prudential" magazine, Newark, N.J., Vol VII. Courtesy Stan Noreika.

Fig. 682

"Some Punkins." Sgnd. Fox. Cover of "Prudential" magazine, Newark N.J., Vol. VII, 3-33, No. 6. 10 x 7 1/2. Courtesy Duane & Dolores Ramsey.

Fig. 683

"Just Arrived." Fox. Cover of "Prudential" magazine, Vol. VI, 2-32, No. 11. 10 x 8. Courtesy Margene & Terry Petros.

Fig. 684

"Worth Protecting." Fox. Cover of "The Prudential" magazine, Vol. VII, 1-33, No. 4. 8 x 7. Courtesy Pat Gibson.

Fig. 685

"Can I Splash?" Fox. Cover of "The Prudential" magazine, Vol. VII, 3-32, No. 3. 8 x 7. Courtesy Pat Gibson

Fig. 686

"Daddy's Hat." Fox. Prudential cover---Vol. VII, No. 2, 2-32. Courtesy Ben & Sandra Ross.

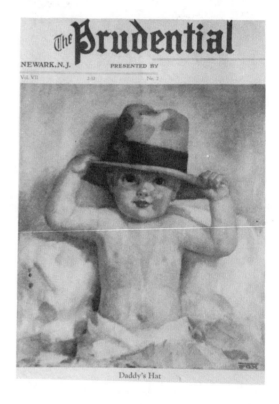

Daddy's Hat

"Shall I Check the Oil?" Fox. Prudential cover, Jan., 1935. 7 1/2 x 6 3/4. Courtesy Pat Gibson.

"Shall I Check the Oil?"

Fig. 688

Fig. 687

ABOUT THE AUTHOR

Rita Mortenson graduated <u>magna cum laude</u> from Central Missouri State University (CMSU) with an undergraduate degree in education and a Master's degree in education and a Master's degree in English. She has also studied art and photography at Longview College and the Kansas City Art Institute and plans to continue her education in the sciences.

She has taught high school and college, dealt in antiques, organized and taught a series of antiques seminars, and worked as "everything from a psychiatric nurse to a model." She has published numerous articles on a variety of subjects and is also the author of prizewinning poems and short stories. In 1980, she published her first article on R. Atkinson Fox and started "Fox Hunt," a collector's newsletter with an audience that increases every year.

In addition to writing, the author is an accomplished photographer and woodcarver. For recreation, she racewalks, bicycles and swims. With her husband, Bob, she enjoys raising butterflies and taking the telescope out for an evening under the stars.

Rita and Bob live in a quiet Kansas City suburb with their sons, Scott, a veterinary student; Alex, who is attending engineering school; one cat; Bob and Scott's show rabbits; and numerous collections. Rita feels fortunate to be able to do so many things she enjoys so much. her full-time work is in the field of Astronomy, and she also teaches Astronomy and English for several area colleges. Colorful Fox prints grace the Mortenson home and the office where Rita compiles her research on Fox and corresponds with "Fox Hunters."

VALUE GUIDE

Values provided here presume a print is in mint or near-mint condition (no wrinkles, tears, stains or fading) and is signed. The frame should be in good condition, representative of the period, and appropriate to the subject matter.

Most values represent prices that have actually been paid at least once. An asterisk (*) beside the "Availability" designation indicates that the print has only been reported by the one source mentioned and, in most cases, has never actually sold on the open market. In these cases, values have been determined by consultation with experienced collectors and dealers.

Values in this book are, across the board, considerably higher than in Book One. Prices have risen rapidly since Book One was published and even since its Value Guide was last revised. More than time and inflation are at work here, however. The prints illustrated in Book One were found over a period of five years of research. Some of the prints in this book have only recently come to light--after nearly twelve years of searching. For the most part, the prints in this book are more scarce--they will be more difficult to find and probably more expensive when they are found--than the prints in Book One.

No one will agree with every value in this book, and that's okay. A number of factors can affect the price a print will bring: geographic area, supply and demand, condition and color of the print, and desirability of the frame, to mention a few. Collectors should remember that the print market is a particularly fickle one (reproductions and "warehouse finds" are but a few of the circumstances that can cause a print's value to plummet). Buy prints because you love them and want to live with them rather than because you hope they will increase in value.

When it has all been said and done, sellers are going to ask what they want for a print and collectors are going to pay what they are willing to pay, regardless of any book. However, a lot of time, effort, research and careful evaluation on the part of a lot of people have gone into this value guide. It is intended to reflect market values, not to set prices. We hope you will find it useful.

Key to Abbreviations Under "Availability":

sc   "scarce"

nc   "not common"

fc   "fairly common"

I eliminated the "highly sought after" (hsa--as in Book One) designation when I found I was applying it to nearly every print.

"Comments" are sometimes something I want to bring to your attention. Sometimes they refer to conditions of a specific sale that figured in the evaluation.

In cases where we do not know size of an example, the print is evaluated as "small" or "medium." "Small" is under 8 x 10. "Medium" prints are at least 8 x 10 but smaller than 16" on any side.

Finally, you will not find a value here for every known size of each print. Simply extrapolate up or down, depending on whether the print in question is larger or smaller than the one listed.

Fig.	Size	Comments	Availability	Value
49	11 x 8		nc	55
50	12 x 24		nc	65
51	7 1/2 x 9 1/2		nc	45
52	11 x 8 1/2	excellent	sc	60
53	10 x 8	excellent	nc	40
54	16 x 10		sc	50
55	9 x 7		nc	45
56	5 1/4 x 3 1/2		nc	40
57	12 x 8		sc	45
58	10 x 8		nc	40
	fan	signed	sc	25
59	20 x 16	must be sgnd. RAF	fc	30
60	18 x 40		sc	80
61	6 x 8		sc	45
62	11 x 8		nc	40
63	6 x 4		sc	40
64	6 x 4	complete calendar	sc	40
65	6 x 4	mint, sepia	sc	45
66	9 x 7	print size	sc	55
67	8 x 11		sc	85
68	14 x 11	excellent	sc	75
69	13 1/2 x 20		nc	65
70	6 x 4	complete calendar	fc	40
		postcard	nc	30
71	8 x 11	unframed	sc	55
72	6 x 4	complete calendar	sc	50
	16 x 10 1/2		nc	65
73	9 x 7		nc	55
74	6 x 5		nc	45
75	11 x 8		nc	55
76	8 1/2 x 6 1/2		nc	40
	blotter			20
77	17 1/2 x 24 1/2		nc	65
78	blotter	mint	sc	20
79	10 x 8		sc	65
80	12 x 9	mint color	nc	50
81	11 x 14	mint	sc	60
82	11 x 14		sc	85
83	3 x 2 1/2		nc	20
84	small to medium		sc	45
85	10 x 8		sc	50
86	4 x 3 1/2		nc	35
87	14 x 20		sc	65
88	medium		sc	85
89	12 x 22		nc	65
90	14 x 28		sc	75
91	6 x 4		nc	40
92	6 x 9		nc	50

Fig.	Size	Comments	Availability	Value
93	6 X 4	complete calendar	sc	40
94	blotter		sc	25
95	6 x 8		nc	35
96	10 x 8	complete calendar	fc	30
97	16 x 10		nc	75
98	14 x 23		nc	65
99	9 x 7		nc	40
100	13 1/2 x 16		nc	50
101	16 x 22	excellent color	sc	100
102	8 x 6	excellent	nc	35
103	8 x 11		fc	35
	13 1/2 x 10	puzzle	nc	65
104	20 x 40		sc	115
105	various-medium		fc	45
106	7 1/2 x 10 1/2		sc	55
107	9 x 7		sc	50
108	11 x 8	excellent	fc	35
109	14 x 22	excellent	fc	35
110	10 x 8		fc	30
111	6 x 8		sc	45
112	complete calendar		nc	25
113	blotter	excellent	nc	20
114	complete calendar		nc	25
115	10 x 8		sc	45
116	5 1/4 x 3 1/2		sc	30
117	5 1/4 x 3 1/2		sc	30
118	5 1/4 x 3 1/2		sc	30
119	5 1/4 x 3 1/2		sc	30
120	5 1/4 x 3 1/2		sc	30
121	5 1/4 x 3 1/2		sc	30
122	5 1/4 x 3 1/2		sc	30
123	5 1/4 x 3 1/2		sc	30
124	6 x 4	complete calendar	sc	40
125	8 3/4 x 5 3/4		sc	45
126	16 x 12		nc	55
127	15 x 10		nc	50
128	14 x 11		sc	55
129	8 1/2 x 12 1/4		sc	55
130	10 1/2 x 7		nc	40
131	10 x 8	excellent	sc	50
132	9 x 13		sc	45
133	5 1/4 x 3 1/2		sc	30
134	medium		sc	50
135	10 x 8		nc	70
136	5 1/4 x 3 1/2		sc	30
137	11 x 8		sc	45
138.	6 x 4	complete calendar	sc	40
139	11 X 8		fc	35

Fig.	Size	Comments	Availability	Value
140	4 x 6		sc	45
141	10 x 8		sc	60
142	7 1/2 x 10 1/2		sc	60
143	12 x 10		sc	65
144	5 1/4 x 3 1/2		sc	40
145	16 x 21		nc	65
146	book page		sc	35
	9 x 12		nc	60
147	6 x 4	unframed	nc	45
148	blotter		nc	25
149	blotter		sc	25
150	10 x 8	excellent	fc	50
	fan		nc	25
151	blotter	excellent	sc	20
152	16 x 12		fc	45
153	12 x 16	questioned-- be sure RAF sig.	fc	25
154	16 x 12		sc	60
155	9 x 12		fc	40
156	10 x 8		nc	50
157	7 x 5		sc	45
158	10 x 6	complete calendar	sc	40
159	7 x 9		sc	50
160	20 x 26		sc	65
161	8 x 10	complete calendar	nc	50
	puzzle		nc	65
162	10 x 8	complete calendar	fc	40
163	11 x 14	excellent color	sc	65
164	5 x 3	excellent	sc	35
165	10 x 8	excellent	nc	55
166	2 3/4 x 3 1/2	on 4 x 9 blotter	nc	35
167	12 x 10		sc	50
168	9 x 6	excellent cond.	sc	45
169	6 x 11 1/2	someone's favorite	sc	70
170	10 x 4		sc	60
171	10 x 8		nc	50
172	6 x 4 1/2		nc	45
173	6 x 4	complete calendar	nc	45
174	10 x 8	mint	fc	40
175	10 x 8	questioned-- be sure RAF sig.	fc	20
176	16 x 12	must be signed RAF	fc	30
177	5 x 7		sc	50
178	6 x 11		sc	85
179	5 x 3	excellent	sc	35
180	10 x 8		nc	90
181	16 x 20		nc	75
182	8 x 10		fc	45

Fig.	Size	Comments	Availability	Value
183	7 x 9		nc	45
184	8 x 11	mint	nc	75
185	14 x 10		fc	65
	fan	3 sections	nc	35
186	12 x 20	unframed	nc	150
187	8 1/2 x 12		nc	110
188	9 1/2 x 12 1/2		nc	125
189	8 x 12		nc	110
190	8 x 12	cut from 1921 newspaper		35
	8 x 10 print	excellent	nc	90
191	5 x 3 1/2	poorly rendered	sc	45
192	9 x 12		nc	85
193	22 x 16		nc	140
194	"medium"		sc	90
195	9 x 12		sc	85
196	16 x 20		sc	125
197	6 x 8	caution-repros.	fc	35
198	7 x 5		sc	55
199	15 x 5		sc	85
200	9 x 7	excellent	sc	85
201	14 x 11		sc	110
202	10 x 8		sc	90
203	15 x 9	unframed calendar	sc	100
204	18 1/2 x 24 1/2		sc	175
205	16 x 22		sc	140
206	15 x 5		sc	65
207	6 x 8	mint	sc	85
208	7 x 10 1/2		sc	125
209	6 x 8		sc	55
210	10 x 8		nc	75
211	6 x 8	mint	sc	65
212	8 x 6	complete calendar	sc	90
213	6 x 8		sc	75
214	16 x 20		nc	125
215	11 x 7 1/2		sc	110
216	7 x 9		nc	90
217	5 x 3	excellent	sc	45
218	7 1/2 x 5 1/2		sc	85
219	5 1/2 x 7 1/2		nc	85
220	7 x 9		sc	90
221	7 x 10		sc	110
222	7 x 9		sc	80
223	14 x 11		sc	100
224	8 x 6	check sig.	sc	65
225	7 1/2 x 10		nc	90
226	6 x 8		nc	100
227	10 1/2 x 7 1/2		sc	140
228	23 x 18	complete calendar	sc	110

Fig.	Size	Comments	Availability	Value
229	8 X 5	complete	sc*	80
230	8 X 5	complete	sc*	80
231	8 x 5	complete	sc*	80
232	8 x 5	complete	sc	80
	blotter			45
233	8 x 5	complete	sc*	80
234	8 x 5	complete	sc*	80
235	8 x 5	complete	sc*	80
236	10 x 5 1/2	complete	sc	80
237	8 x 5	complete	sc*	80
238	8 x 5	complete	sc*	80
239	8 x 5	complete	sc*	80
240	11 x 8	mint	nc	75
241		complete	sc*	90
242		complete	sc*	110
243		complete	sc*	90
244		complete	sc*	90
245		complete	sc*	110
246		complete	sc*	90
247		complete	sc*	90
248		complete	sc*	90
249		complete	sc*	90
250		complete	sc*	90
251		complete	sc*	90
252		complete	sc*	110
253		unframed		70
253	9 x 7		nc	100
	fan		sc	35
254		"medium"		90
255	9 x 7		nc	90
256	10 1/4 x 8 1/2		nc	75
257	9 x 12		nc	75
258	medium		nc	75
259	4 1/2 x 12	from scrapbook	sc	105
260	15 x 9	unframed calendar		100
261	6 1/2 x 10		sc	90
262	6 x 8	faces poorly done	nc	75
263	9 1/2 x 7		nc	90
264	2 3/4 x 2		nc	65
265	13 x 10		nc	90
266	5 x 7			125
267	8 x 7		nc	90
268	6 x 8		sc	115
269	14 x 11		sc	100
270	medium		sc	90
271	9 x 6		sc	90
272	11 x 8 1/2		sc	100
273	7 1/3 x 10 1/4		nc	100

Fig.	Size	Comments	Availability	Value
274	9 x 3		sc	75
275	9 x 3		sc	65
276	16 1/2 x 9		sc*	125
277	medium		sc	100
278	medium		sc*	110
279	16 x 11	complete calendar	nc	100
	14 x 10	puzzle	nc	90
280	9 x 7	from scrapbook	sc	85
281	8 1/4 x 11 1/4		sc	140
282	8 x 6	complete calendar	nc	55
283	medium		sc	100
284	11 x 8		sc	95
285	8 x 6		sc	100
286	10 x 8	complete calendar	nc	75
287	medium		nc	90
288	21 x 17		nc	110
289	14 x 9 1/2		nc	100
290	10 x 8		nc	75
291	11 x 14	excellent	fc	60
	Harbor Villa puzzle		nc	75
	Perfect Double puzzle		sc	125
292	9 x 14		fc	70
293	9 x 12	excellent	fc	65
294	14 x 10 1/2		nc	90
295	8 1/2 x 6		sc*	95
296	3 x 5		sc*	110
297	11 x 9		sc	100
298	8 x 6		sc	125
299	9 x 4 1/2		nc	85
300	8 x 10		nc	75
301	7 x 9		nc	75
302	22 x 28		sc	175
303	6 x 8		sc	90
304	11 x 8 1/2		sc	125
305	postcard		sc	40
306	11 x 11	mint	sc	140
307	11 x 8		sc	135
308	13 x 10		nc	140
309	8 x 6		sc	175
	16 x 20			300
310	11 x 8		sc	130
311	15 x 9		sc	150
312	medium		sc	100
313	6 1/2 x 8 1/2		sc	100
314	5 1/4 x 3 3/4		sc	80
315	11 1/2 x 8 1/2		sc	100
316	9 x 6		sc	90
317	11 x 8		sc	100

Fig.	Size	Comments	Availability	Value
317 cont.	greeting card	mint	sc	25
318	6 x 8		sc	100
319	9 x 7		sc	115
320	9 3/4 x 7 3/4		sc	90
321	9 x 11 1/2		sc	100
322	7 x 5		sc	75
323	5 x 4		nc	80
324	10 x 8		nc	100
325	7 x 10		sc	110
326	12 x 8		sc	110
327	10 x 8		sc	100
328	12 x 9		nc	80
329	8 x 6		nc	80
330	20 1/2 x 13 1/2		nc	140
331	12 x 8		nc	90
332	11 x 8		sc*	125
333	8 x 11	complete calendar	sc	125
334	11 x 8		sc	140
335	7 x 5		sc	50
336	12 x 11		sc	70
337	19 x 14		nc	125
338	4 1/2 x 8 1/2		sc*	90
339	9 x 12		sc	110
340	9 1/2 x 7 1/2	portion	sc	65
341	8 1/4 x 12		sc	80
342	20 x 15		nc	125
	6 x 4	mint color	nc	45
343		tray	nc	80
344	12 1/2 x 8 1/2		sc	90
345	12 x 9		fc	75
345	10 1/2 x 7		sc	75
347	9 x 7		nc	75
348	20 x 16	excellent	nc	125
349	8 x 6 1/2		sc	75
350	15 x 12 1/2		sc	110
351	21 x 15	complete calendar	fc	110
352	8 x 12		nc	85
353	9 x 12		sc	100
354	8 x 12		fc	65
354-a	8 x 6 portion			50
355	5 x 11		sc	75
356	9 x 7	mint	sc	75
357	6 x 8	excellent condition	sc	90
358	17 x 14		sc	125
359	10 x 8		sc	110
360	5 x 7	unframed	sc	85
361	13 1/2 x 9 1/2		sc*	175
362	10 x 8		fc	90

Fig.	Size	Comments	Availability	Value
363	9 x 5	excellent color	sc	125
364	8 x 6		sc	65
365	12 x 18		sc	110
366	16 x 20		sc	100
367	10 1/2 x 7 5/8	check signature	sc	75
368	6 x 8 1/2		sc	65
369	13 x 5		sc	90
370	7 1/2 x 10		sc	80
371	9 x 12		fc	65
372	7 x 11		sc	75
373	14 x 10		sc	90
374	8 1/4 x 11 1/2		sc	85
375	8 x 10		nc	65
376	3 1/2 x 5		sc	45
377	3 1/2 x 5		sc	45
378	7 x 10	complete calendar	nc	80
379	7 x 10		sc	80
380	15 x 5	excellent	fc	75
381	7 x 9		fc	75
382	postcard		sc	20
383	medium		sc	75
384	6 1/2 x 10		sc	75
385	9 1/2 x 13 1/2		nc	90
	11 x 16 puzzle		sc	90
386	14 x 11	mint	fc	70
	7 x 5	thermometer		45
387	5 x 7		fc	65
388	5 x7		sc	65
389	8 x 10		sc	80
390	5 1/2 x 10 1/2		sc	75
391	7 x 5		sc	75
	on Buster Brown cal.		sc	100
392	10 x 8		nc	80
393	medium		nc	90
394	12 x 16		sc	110
395	6 x 8		sc	75
396	medium		sc*	100
397	5 x 7		sc	80
398	8 x 6		sc	65
399	8 1/4 x 6 1/4		sc	65
400	5 x 7		nc	50
401	5 1/2 x 7 3/4		sc*	80
402	5 3/4 x 7 1/3		sc	60
403	10 x 16		nc	90
404	medium		sc	65
405	6 x 8		nc	60
406	3 1/2 x 5		sc	45
407	16 x 13 1/2		sc	100

Fig.	Size	Comments	Availability	Value
408	8 x 11		sc	80
409	12 x 9		sc	80
410	7 x 10 1/2		sc	65
411	12 x 16		sc	110
412	7 x 10	excellent	sc	65
413	8 x 10			100
414	6 x 4		nc	40
415	5 x 15		sc	95
416	7 1/2 x 10 1/2		sc	100
417	8 1/2 x 12 1/2		sc	90
418	4 x 10	excellent color	sc	110
419	6 x 8		sc	65
420	8 x 10		nc	65
421	8 x 6		sc	80
422	7 1/2 x 9 1/2		nc	75
423	8 x 6		nc	110
424	6 x 8		sc	75
425	12 x 8		sc	90
426	9 x 7		nc	65
427	9 x 12	excellent	sc	80
428	medium		sc	75
429	5 x 7		nc	80
430	6 x 8	puzzle		80
431	5 1/2 x 8		sc	65
432	medium		sc	75
433	9 x 12	excellent	fc	55
	15 7/8 x 20			80
436	11 x 8		sc	75
437	5 x 7 1/2		sc	55
438	8 x 12		nc	65
439	11 x 8		fc	65
440	8 x 4		nc	95
441	10 x 8	excellent	nc	90
443	14 x 21	mint	sc	135
444	6 x 8		nc	80
445	9 x 12	excellent	nc	100
446	14 1/2 x 10		sc	200
447	10 x 8		sc	90
448	14 x 12		nc	100
449	medium		sc*	125
450	6 x 8		nc	75
451	9 x 7		sc	85
	16 x 12		nc	100
453	6 x 4	complete calendar	sc	60
454	8 x 12		fc	65
455	6 x 8	complete calendar	sc	75
456	11 x 8	complete calendar	nc	75
457	8 x 12		nc	75

Fig.	Size	Comments	Availability	Value
458	9 x 13		nc	75
459	3 1/2 x 3 1/3		nc	45
461	15 x 5	complete calendar	sc	110
462	10 1/2 x 11		nc	85
463	10 1/2 x 10		nc	85
464	7 x 11	complete calendar	sc	105
465	10 x 15		nc	115
466	6 x 12		sc	90
467	9 x 6		sc	90
468	10 x 8		nc	80
469	15 x 5		sc	110
470	16 x 22 1/2		sc	125
471	small		sc*	80
472	11 1/2 x 9		nc	75
473	11 x 10		sc	90
474	11 x 8	excellent	nc	75
475	8 x 10	sepia	sc	75
476	8 x 20	excellent	sc	95
477	?		sc*	85+
478	13 x 18	excellent	nc	85
479	6 x 8		sc	75
480	?		sc*	85+

* Note: Prints marked with an asterisk (*) by their "availability" designation (AVL: sc, e.g.) have only been reported by the one source mentioned: The People's Art Project, a Thos. D. Murphy catalog, The Red Wing Paintings Book, etc.

FL#	Index By Fox-List Number	Fig. #
487	"Yosemite Falls"	133
488	"Mirror Lake"	121
489	"Grand Canyon"	118
490	"Lower Falls--Yellowstone Park"	136
491	"Pike's Peak"	119
492	"Glacier Nat'l Park"	120
493	"Lookout Mountain"	122
494	"The Dells of Wisconsin"	123
495	"Thousand Islands"	56
496	"Palisades of the Hudson"	144
497	Untitled	417
498	Untitled	374
499	Untitled	326
500	"Valley of Enchantment, The"	297
501	Untitled	271
502	"Returning From Pasture"	373
503	Untitled	222
504	"Busy Mill, The"	169
505	"Where Memories Stray"	151
506	"Just Before Sunrise"	115
507	"Browsing"	405
508	Untitled	95
509	"Challenge, The"	459
510	Untitled	422
511	"Pals"	349
512	"Thoroughbreds"	323
513	"Treat, The"	322
514	"Monarch of the North"	461
515	"Sunset in the Big North Woods"	462
516	Untitled	448
517	"Ruth"	304
518	"In a Lovely Garden..."	155
519	Untitled	163
520	"It's Only a Cottage, But It's Home"	161
521	"Three Twins, The"	418
522	"In New York Bay"	149
523	Untitled	73
524	"Mount Rainier"	72
525	"Mount LeFroy"	86
526	"Sunrise, Coast of Maine"	140
527	"Last of the Herd, The"	465

FL#	Index By Fox-List Number	Fig. #
528	"Washington at Valley Forge"	188
529	"Peaceful Day, A"	414
530	"Mount of the Holy Cross--Colo."	70
531	"Nature's Sentinels"	62
532	"Peaceful Valley"	474
533	"Faithful and True"	218
534	"Best Piemaker in Town, The"	219
535	"Mountain Lake"	104
536	Untitled	404
538	"Old Mill, The"	174
539	"Thoroughbreds"	403
540	"Close of Day, The"	399
541	"Where Peace Abides"	110
542	"Sunrise"	57
543	"Silvery Pathway, A"	168
544	"Departure of Columbus"	187
545	"Gosh"	224
546	Untitled	319
547	"Reward, The"	320
548	Untitled	210
549	"Fury of the Flames"	454
550	"In Full Chase"	431
551	Untitled	82
552	Untitled	357
553	"Good Morning"	340
554	"At the Fountain"	347
555	"Chewing the Cud"	402
556	Untitled	372
557	"Aces All"	180
558	"Dreamland"	157
559	"Sunset in Normandy"	145
560	"Moonlight at the Camp"	53
561	Untitled	51
562	"Curfew Tolls the Knell of Parting Day, The"	177
563	"Mill and the Birches, The"	171
564	"Vernal Falls"	137
565	"The Sky Line"	255
567	"Golden West"	131
568	"Pure and Healthful"	106
569	"Cool and Refreshing"	142
570	"A Golden Sunset"	107

FL# or Other Signature	Alphabetical Index of Print Titles	Fig. #
463	("Flight to Egypt")	185
Turner	"'Neath Sunset Skies"	646
Atkins	"A Day in the Open"	680
570	"A Golden Sunset"	107
763	"A Native Son"	449
473	"Aberdeen Angus"	406
700	"Abraham Lincoln"	240
740	"Abraham Lincoln"	229
557	"Aces All"	180
DeForest	"Adventuress, The"	572
407	"After a Day's Work"	355
356	"After the Harvest"	183
388	"After the Harvest"	182
690	"After the Harvest"	471
Musson	"After the Harvest"	639
DeForest	"Age of Innocence"	580
GBF	"Alert"	539
758	"Alexander Bell"	249
White	"All Set"	675
Dupre	"Aloya of the South Seas"	592
695	"America's Breadbasket"	470
664	"American Madonna"	288
684	"Among the Daisies"	273
709	"An Armful of Joy"	286
Musson	"An Interesting Family"	644
653	"An Uninvited Guest"	453
743	"Andrew Carnegie"	232
742	"Andrew Jackson"	231
Fox?	"Anxious Moments"	679-a
589	"Anxious Mother, The"	440
GBF	"Aristocrat, The"	547
403	"As the Sun Goes Down"	386
Lewis	"Asters"	625
Musson	"At Eventide"	632
Dupre	"At Peace With the World"	596
Wain	"At Sundown in the Golden West"	652
GBF	"At the Close of Day"	524
332	"At the Foot Hills of Pike's Peak"	99
White	"At the Foot of Mount Rainier"	668

FL# or Other Signature	Alphabetical Index of Print Titles	Fig. #
554	"At the Fountain"	347
579	"At the Pool"	370
666	"Attractions of the Farm"	310
449	"Autumn Glow"	60
GBF	"Awaiting the Call"	542
630	"Baby's First Tooth"	289
342	"Barefoot Boy, The"	280
DeForest	"Barrel of Fun, A"	586
Lewie	"Battle Royal, A"	616
Wain	"Being Helpful"	665
744	"Benjamin Franklin"	233
534	"Best Piemaker in Town, The"	219
671	"Between Two Fires"	221
660	"Birch-Bordered Waters"	108
696	"Blue Ribbon Pair, A"	365
474	"Bonnie J. International Champion"	376
DeForest	"Bounty from Heaven, A"	579
337	"Bred in the Purple"	354
507	"Browsing"	405
Fox?	"Buddies"	682
617	"Bunch of Beauties"	413
400	"Busy Mill, The"	170
504	"Busy Mill, The"	169
Wood	"By a Falling Crystal Stream"	676
719	"By the Campfire Glow"	206
394	"By the Old Mill Stream"	175
Dupre	"By the Zuider Zee"	593
404	"By Winding Stream"	387
677	"Call, The"	464
Wain	"Campers, The"	653
Fox?	"Can I Spash"	686
393	"Canyon, The"	66
509	"Challenge, The"	459
699	"Challenge, The"	443
GBF	"Challenger, The"	546
GBF	"Champion, The"	545
454	"Champions of the West"	408
555	"Chewing the Cud"	402
Dupre	"Chieftain's Pride"	590

FL# or Other Signature	Alphabetical Index of Print Titles	Fig. #
DeForest	"Childhood Days"	582
DeForest	"Children's Hour, The"	574
Colvin	"Chums"	559
606	"Clear Creek Canyon--Colo."	93
Colvin	"Close Friends"	567
540	"Close of Day, The"	399
658	"Colorado Canyon"	83
409	"Columbia River--Oregon"	87
641	"Come Along My Beauty"	211
628	"Companions"	314
458	"Contentment"	378
569	"Cool and Refreshing"	142
412	"Cottage by the Sea, The"	167
432	"Cottage by the Sea"	143
483	"Country Road"	400
Carr	"Cozy Cottage"	557
Lewis	"Critical Moment, A"	613
657	"Crystal Falls"	166
562	"Curfew Tolls the Knell of Parting Day, The"	177
755	"Cyrus McCormick"	246
Fox?	"Daddy's Hat"	687
410	"Day Dreams"	291
626	"Day's Work Done, The"	356
341	"Deering"	330
544	"Departure of Columbus"	187
GBF	"Diplomat, The"	548
395	"Discovery of the Mississippi, 1541"	186
Lewis	"Discretion is the Better Part of Valor"	609
Colvin	"Disputed Property"	564
384	"Down by the Bridge"	282
668	"Down Memory Lane"	158
701	"Down on Grandpa's Farm"	215
436	"Dream Castle"	290
GBF	"Dream Garden"	526
558	"Dreamland"	157
329	"Dreamy Paradise"	152
Dupre	"Dreamy Valley"	595
688	"Duke"	336
GBF	"Eager For Action"	536

FL# or Other Signature	Alphabetical Index of Print Titles	Fig. #
Wain	"Echoing Call, The"	654
754	"Eli Whitney"	245
752	"Elias Howe"	243
385	"Emperor, The"	364
GBF	"Enchanted Pool, The"	528
674	"End of the Trail"	78
DeForest	"Esmerelda"	576
381	"Evening in the Mountains"	456
691	"Evening"	401
Musson	"Evening"	631
Lewis	"Ever Watchful"	608
364	"Fair Skipper, A"	299
593	"Fairy-like Vision, A"	101
621	"Faith"	272
533	"Faithful and True"	218
656	"Faithful and True"	312
397	"Faithful Friends"	327
Colvin	"Faithful Guardian, A"	558
GBF	"Faithful to His Trust"	533
Colvin	"Faithful"	563
Musson	"Farm Yard, The"	633
469	"Fascinating"	334
GBF	"Favorite Spot, A"	523
Wain	"Favorite, The"	663
425	"First Raising of the Stars & Stripes..."	190
465	"First Tourists Visit Old Faithful"	203
682	"Fish Story, The"	283
Wain	"Flavor of Fall, The"	649
376	"Flower of the Forest"	253
581	"Fooling Him"	318
645	"Fording the Stream"	363
355	"Forest Ranger, The"	200
Musson	"Four of a Kind"	643
Wain	"Fra Longfellow Glen"	655
431	"Fraternally Yours"	342
365	"Friendly Greeting"	350
464	"Friends"	348
582	"Friends"	315
549	"Fury of the Flames"	454

FL# or Other Signature	Alphabetical Index of Print Titles	Fig. #
648	"Future Prize Winners	416
633	"Gage's Surrender"	189
679	"Golden Gate"	154
Carr	"Garden Home, The"	553
Wain	"Garden of Flowers, A"	658
598	"Gates of Dreamland, The"	294
328	"General 'Mad' Anthony Wayne..."	192
751	"George Stevenson"	242
729	"Getting Together"	415
382	"Geyser"	49
366	"Giant Steps Falls"	139
574	"Girl of the Golden West, The"	316
White	"Girl of the Golden West, The"	671
492	"Glacier Nat'l Park"	120
333	"Glorious Solitude, A"	67
715	"Glory of Youth"	309
362	"Going to the Fire"	361
GBF	"Golden & Sunny & Filled With Good Cheer..."	517
567	"Golden West"	131
627	"Good Luck"	335
553	"Good Morning"	340
345	"Good News"	199
545	"Gosh"	224
489	"Grand Canyon"	118
Dupre	"Grandeur of Nature"	594
Carr	"Grandeur of Summer, The"	555
GBF	"Great Outdoors, The"	503
Lewis	"Grip of Winter, The"	619
711	"Grover Cleveland"	236
591	"Guardian of the Valley"	103
GBF	"Guardian, The"	549
Lewis	"Guardian, The"	601
750	"Gutenberg"	241
451	"Harvesting"	360
Carr	"Haven of Splendor, A"	556
DeForest	"He Loves Me, He Loves Me Not"	581
358	"Heart of the Seilkerts"	91
447	"Heights of Quebec, The"	147
447	"Heights of Quebec, The"	148

FL# or Other Signature	Alphabetical Index of Print Titles	Fig. #
375	"Her Pet"	328
471	"Herefords"	394
730	"Herefords, The"	393
586	"Hero of the Alps"	421
618	"High Noon"	369
344	"His First Lesson"	359
GBF	"Home of Happy Memories, A"	520
423	"Home of the West Wind, The"	98
411	"Homeward Bound"	173
692	"Homeward Bound"	477
Musson	"Homeward Bound"	637
DeForest	"Honest and Truly"	585
739	"Horse Pasture, The"	338
GBF	"House by the Side of the Road, The"	511
Wain	"House by the Side of the Road, The"	659
518	"In a Lovely Garden..."	155
550	"In Full Chase"	431
437	"In Full Cry"	432
577	"In Green Pastures"	479
522	"In New York Bay"	149
703	"In the Days of '49"	262
631	"In the Foothills"	261
418	"In the Heart of the Sierra Nevadas"	127
373	"In the Jungle"	452
578	"In the Meadow Pasture"	371
408	"In the Pasture Stream"	388
430	"In the Pasture"	392
Musson	"In the Pasture"	627
Fox?	"Indian at Prayer"	677
710	"Iron Horse, The--Driving the Golden Spike"	204
520	"It's Only a Cottage, But It's Home"	161
746	"James J. Hill"	235
753	"James Watt"	244
764	"Jerseys"	396
702	"Journey's End, The--Oregon"	205
615	"Juleposten I Nordlandet"	423
349	"Just a Place to Call Our Own"	159
Fox?	"Just Arrived"	684
506	"Just Before Sunrise"	115

FL# or Other Signature	Alphabetical Index of Print Titles	Fig. #
610	"Kap Nome, Alaska"	141
GBF	"Keen Pair, A"	540
GBF	"King of the Hunt"	544
676	"Kingdom of the Wild"	455
402	"Lake Louise--Alberta"	81
Dupre	"Land of Sky Blue Waters"	591
737	"Land Where the Mountains are Nameless..."	125
527	"Last of the Herd, The"	465
433	"Leader, The"	473
638	"Life Saver, A"	277
GBF	"Little Gardener"	530
734	"Lone Eagle, The"	226
597	"Look Pretty"	284
493	"Lookout Mountain"	122
GBF	"Lovely as a Dream of June Time"	512
490	"Lower Falls--Yellowstone Park"	136
Lewis	"Lure of the Lake, The"	621
330	"Magic Forest"	80
572	"Maid in the U.S.A."	333
Wain	"Maid in U.S.A."	664
GBF	"Majestic Nature"	496
476	"Majesty of Nature, The"	71
Musson	"Making a Dicker"	636
326	"Man and Beast Prepare Land..."	358
760	"Marconi"	251
745	"Marshall Field"	234
Lewis	"Master of All He Surveys"	603
596	"Maud Muller"	305
Wain	"Me and Dixie"	662
681	"Me and Rex"	278
GBF	"Meadowbrook"	501
467	"Meditation"	307
716	"Meditation"	295
718	"Mid Flowers Fair"	303
391	"Mid Mountain Verdure"	102
DeForest	"Mighty Like a Rose"	578
563	"Mill and the Birches, The"	171
488	"Mirror Lake"	121
Lewis	"Monarch of All He Surveys"	604

FL# or Other Signature	Alphabetical Index of Print Titles	Fig. #
514	"Monarch of the North"	461
613	"Monarch of the North"	446
GBF	"Monarch of the North"	506
Wilson	"Monarch of the Wilderness"	668-a
728	"Monarch, The"	463
460	"Monarchs of the Prairie"	379
442	"Monarchs, The"	444
560	"Moonlight at the Camp"	53
481	"Morning Call, The"	457
DeForest	"Mother's Darling"	577
721	"Mother's Joy"	285
525	"Mount LeFroy"	86
377	"Mount Lindbergh"	97
530	"Mount of the Holy Cross--Colo."	70
485	"Mount Rainier"	116
524	"Mount Rainier"	72
486	"Mount Shasta"	117
607	"Mount Shasta--California"	124
604	"Mount Sir Donald--Canada"	64
413	"Mountain Glow"	74
535	"Mountain Lake"	104
440	"Mountain Majesty"	114
GBF	"Mountain Stream, The"	497
387	"Mountain Trail, The"	68
324	"Mt. Rainier Glowing in Rosy Splendor"	100
720	"Mutual Affections"	287
398	"My Boy"	220
738	"My Castle of Dreams"	292
343	"Mystic Hour, The"	52
390	"Nature's Grandeur"	111
475	"Nature's Hidden Places"	58
531	"Nature's Sentinels"	62
659	"New England Coast, A"	88
Fox?	"Next to Nature's Heart"	679
735	"Night Call, The"	458
348	"Northward Bound"	468
713	"October Sport"	430
Turner	"Off New England Shores"	645
708	"Oh Susanna--The Covered Wagon"	213

FL# or Other Signature	Alphabetical Index of Print Titles	Fig. #
603	"Old Bridge, The"	164
389	"Old Faithful by Moonlight"	260
620	"Old Faithful"	478
Wain	"Old Fishing Hole, The"	661
601	"Old Meeting House, The"	179
538	"Old Mill, The"	174
602	"Old Mill, The"	217
693	"Old Mill, The"	172
GBF	"Old Mill, The"	516
Lewis	"Old Ocean Roars, The Jungle Answers"	606
Wain	"Old Pathway, The"	650
Lewis	"On a Trail"	612
588	"On Guard"	436
Colvin	"On Guard"	561
Lewis	"On Rocky Heights"	615
346	"On the Alert"	438
Lewis	"On the Lookout"	611
359	"On the Meadows"	384
White	"On the Trail"	673
732	"On the Way to the Mill"	92
DeForest	"On Treasure Isle"	573
Wain	"One Hundred Percent (100%) Pure"	660
683	"One Strike"	276
478	"Open Season"	424
669	"Oriental Beauties"	300
575	"Oriental Dreams"	293
736	"Out of the Sky He Comes"	227
GBF	"Out Where the West Begins"	509
Wain	"Overlooking Emerald Bay"	651
GBF	"Pair of Beauties, A"	529
GBF	"Pal O' Mine"	550
496	"Palisades of the Hudson"	144
511	"Pals"	349
438	"Paradise Bay"	112
Wain	"Paradise Valley"	656
452	"Pasture Lane, The"	380
592	"Path to Home, The"	61
654	"Peace and Contentment"	367
529	"Peaceful Day, A"	414

FL# or Other Signature	Alphabetical Index of Print Titles	Fig. #
532	"Peaceful Valley"	474
704	"Peaceful Valley"	391
DeForest	"Perfect Melody, A"	575
748	"Philip D. Armour"	238
491	"Pike's Peak"	119
611	"Pike's Peak..Garden of the Gods"	77
352	"Pioneer, The"	198
Colvin	"Playmates"	562
DeForest	"Playmates"	583
585	"Please Don't Make Us Go To Bed"	267
649	"Pointer, The"	425
GBF	"Poised for Action"	541
608	"Popocatapel--Mexico"	63
594	"Port of Heart's Desire, The"	150
686	"Portrait of George Washington"	228
622	"Prepared"	281
426	"Prides of the West"	420
479	"Prize Stock"	375
415	"Prize Winners"	389
472	"Prize Winners"	377
435	"Prosperity"	381
GBF	"Protected"	505
568	"Pure and Healthful"	106
762	"Purebred Herd"	480
733	"Purple Majesty"	105
Wain	"Quiet Solitude"	667
?	"Ramona"	591-a
573	"Ready for a Cantor"	317
428	"Ready for All Comers"	337
667	"Reliable Guardian, A"	433
640	"Repairing of All Kinds"	265
636	"Rest Haven"	162
502	"Returning From Pasture"	373
547	"Reward, The"	320
482	"Right of Way, The"	197
396	"Ring Around Rosy"	266
756	"Robert Fulton"	247
468	"Roses Fair"	308
331	"Rosy Glow of the Land of Promise"	76

FL# or Other Signature	Alphabetical Index of Print Titles	Fig. #
714	"Spirit of Discovery"	225
706	"Spirit of the Harvest"	298
650	"Startled"	466
GBF	"Steamboat 'Round the Bend"	551
420	"Stony Mill in Spring" (Westal)	176
Lewis	"Strength and Security"	598
Lewis	"Strength"	614
DeForest	"Strictly Confidential"	588
GBF	"Strike, A"	521
406	"Summer Day, A"	410
350	"Summertime at Grandpa's"	184
422	"Sunland"	109
542	"Sunrise"	57
526	"Sunrise, Coast of Maine"	140
559	"Sunset in Normandy"	145
515	"Sunset in the Big North Woods"	462
GBF	"Sunset in the North Woods"	522
614	"Supreme"	445
685	"Sweet Memories"	306
644	"Taking a Trench"	196
DeForest	"Teasing"	584
357	"Tense Moment, A"	428
GBF	"Tense Point, A"	538
360	"The Artist Supreme"	135
494	"The Dells of Wisconsin"	123
652	"The Great Divide"	129
673	"The Mountain in All Its Glory"	130
565	"The Sky Line"	255
642	"Their Attack Conquered"	207
Colvin	"Their First Lesson"	565
Colvin	"Their Great Day"	566
741	"Theodore Roosevelt"	230
456	"There's a Light in the Window..."	194
759	"Thomas Edison"	250
Musson	"Thoroughbred, A"	642
512	"Thoroughbreds"	323
539	"Thoroughbreds"	403
495	"Thousand Islands"	56
724	"Three Friends"	332

FL# or Other Signature	Alphabetical Index of Print Titles	Fig. #
587	"Three Pals, The"	427
521	"Three Twins, The"	418
643	"Thrilling Moment, A"	313
726	"Thrills Afield"	426
466	"Through the Mountain Pass"	202
583	"Tom and Jerry"	339
GBF	"Tom, Dick and Harry"	532
480	"Top Notchers"	419
GBF	"Tranquility"	510
361	"Treasure Fleet, The"	146
GBF	"Treasure Ship, The"	552
383	"Treat, A"	321
513	"Treat, The"	322
327	"Turn of the Tide, The..."	195
427	"U.S.A. Quality"	412
Wain	"Unbroken Bond of Frienship"	666
Wain	"Under the Greenwood Tree"	648
Musson	"Under the Maples"	638
Lewis	"Untamed Monarchs"	610
500	"Valley of Enchantment, The"	297
564	"Vernal Falls"	137
605	"Vernal falls--Yosemite, California"	138
Wain	"View Through the Timber, A"	647
725	"Vigilance"	439
595	"Village Belle, The"	302
Musson	"Waiting for Orders"	641
484	"Waiting for Their Master"	441
Dupre	"Wanetah"	589
637	"Warm Friends"	279
749	"Warren Harding"	239
Wain	"Washington & LaFayette at Valley Forge"	666-a
Lewis	"Washington at Headquarters"	617
Lewis	"Washington at the Battle of Monmouth	618
528	"Washington at Valley Forge"	188
712	"Washington at Valley Forge"	191
Carr	"Watching"	554
717	"Water Lilies"	296
453	"Watering Place, The"	382
GBF	"What Price Pal?"	534

FL# or Other Signature	Alphabetical Index of Print Titles	Fig. #
353	"When Evening Calls Them Home"	383
439	"When Evening Shadows Fall"	113
GBF	"When Seconds Count"	507
Musson	"When the Cows Come Home"	628
399	"When the Day is Over"	165
392	"Where Brooks Send Up a Cheerful Tune"	223
GBF	"Where Dreams Come True"	515
405	"Where Giants Wrought"	65
505	"Where Memories Stray"	151
445	"Where Peace Abides"	55
541	"Where Peace Abides"	110
698	"Who Said Dinner?"	353
761	"Wilbur Wright"	252
461	"Wild Life"	467
661	"Winding River, The"	94
368	"Witching Hour, The"	54
441	"With Dog and Gun"	429
455	"Woodland and Cattle"	407
420	"Woodland Brook" (Wood)	176
Fox?	"Worth Protecting"	685
487	"Yosemite Falls"	133
722	"You Shan't Go Swimming, So There!"	264
	FL# or Other Signature / Alphabetical Index of Print Titles / Fig. #